EARTH
ELDER
STORIES

EARTH
ELDER
STORIES

THE PINAYZITT PATH

ALEXANDER WOLFE

FIFTH
HOUSE

The publisher gratefully acknowledges the support of The Canada Council for the Arts and the Department of Canadian Heritage.

THE CANADA COUNCIL | LE CONSEIL DES ARTS
FOR THE ARTS | DU CANADA
SINCE 1957 | DEPUIS 1957

We acknowledge the financial support of the Government of Canada through the Book Publishing Industry Development Program for our publishing activities.

Printed in Canada

02 03 04 05 06/ 7 6 5 4 3

CANADIAN CATALOGUING IN PUBLICATION DATA

Wolfe, Alexander, 1927–2002
Earth Elder Stories: the Pinayzitt path
ISBN: 0-920079-35-0

1. Ojibwa Indians—Anecdotes*. 2. Ojibwa Indians—History*.   I. Title
E99.C6W65   1988   970.004'97   C88 007506-6

Cover and interior illustrations by Henry Standing Alone
Design by Articulate Eye Design

Published in Canada by
Fifth House Ltd.
A Fitzhenry & Whiteside Company
1511-1800 4 Street SW
Calgary, Alberta, Canada
T2S 2S5
1-800-387-9776
www.fitzhenry.ca

First published in the US in 2002.

CONTENTS

PREFACE

To mainstream North American society, and to aboriginal people who have become isolated from their culture, Indian oral tradition may seem to be a thing of the past. The few legends that persist in written form today are regarded as merely relics of that past and are believed to constitute the totality of oral tradition. But if one enters Indian society today, especially where the Native language is still widely or exclusively spoken, it soon becomes apparent that oral stories abound in various forms. Legends are but one aspect of a living tradition in which also exist histories, ceremonial stories, healing stories, and humorous tales and anecdotes. Oral tradition is still an important and integral part of Indian societies.

Alex Wolfe is a knowledgeable representative and product of this tradition. He is an oral historian, a keeper of his family's history, one of the first to commit his stories to a written, published form. His purpose in taking this enormous step is to reach out to those who have lost their culture and are searching to restore the missing pieces to their identity. The underlying message of his work is that the way to know who we are today and the strength to face our uncertain future lies in knowing our past—our history. It is his hope that other storytellers will record their families' histories.

Wolfe's work is significant in that it is a written presentation of authentic Indian history. His book contains many of the important elements of the traditional Indian approach to history. He presents historical accounts in narrative form, interwoven with the significant events, personalities, and notable places, such as the ancestral homeland and sacred pilgrimage sites of his people. Historiographical elements such as a genealogy and maps are presented to support these accounts and to serve other important traditional functions as well. A clan's genealogy was essential for determining the procreation of healthy offspring and thereby ensuring their survival. Geographical knowledge of plains, lakes, rivers, and mountain ranges was crucial to their survival because it was on these vast areas that they roamed, hunting and gathering food, evading and confronting their traditional enemies.

Wolfe's book will serve as a starting point and a guide in the development of written histories of indigenous peoples. Wolfe's work is testimony to the vast, untapped knowledge of history and culture that exists in our own back yard. It is hoped that it will encourage Indian educators and scholars to turn their attention to this traditional source of knowledge and begin the long and arduous task of using it to develop a knowledge base of authentic Indian history and philosophy that will be an original product of their academic institutions. Finally, the stories are presented in written form to society as a whole to offer an insight into an untold history of North America.

Wolfe's stories are windows into this dynamic past, through which one witnesses the epic and supernatural history that now seems alien and unbelievable to the modern viewer. But the countryside of southern Saskatchewan is filled with the richness of that history, embedded in its trees, hills, and vast plains. It is on this very land that the *Pinayzitt* people roamed and many wonderful and many tragic events took place. It was here that the stories and songs were made and remembered by the grand-fathers and grandmothers who participated in those events. They wanted their stories and songs passed on to future generations.

Here now we have some of those stories, and in them we can see the social, political, spiritual, and economic life of a people struggling to withstand the relentless encroachment of an alien and hostile force. The very psyche of a people is revealed in Wolfe's accounts, in their hardships, joy, commitments, and challenges. His stories reveal man's interdependent relationship with his environment, his responsibility to himself, to his fellow man and to all of creation. In his descriptions and explanations, Wolfe provides insight into not only how things were done but why they were done. The stories are not merely a presentation of "dry" material facts of history, they also convey the deeply philosophical and spiritual aspects of that history.

Because Indian oral tradition blends the material, spiritual, and philosophical together into one historical entity, it would be a clear violation of the culture from which it is derived if well-meaning scholars were to try to demythologize it, in order to give it greater validity in the Western sense of historiography. It would be equally unjust and inappropriate to place this history into the category of mythology or folklore, thereby stripping it of its significance as authentic historical documentation.

There is a correct and respectful approach to oral traditions, which Wolfe recommends in his introduction. It is important to reiterate his points briefly. First, to gain a deeper understanding of history and culture through the stories of its people one must first learn the language of the family, tribe, or nation to which the stories belong. Language and culture are inextricably interwoven and interdependent. Second, in approaching oral traditions one must become aware of the principles and prac tices that govern those traditions. Just as Western literary traditions have their modes and devices, and history its established methodologies, Indian oral traditions have rules and principles that are distinct and valid in their own right. Third, it should be recognized that the practice and principles of oral traditions vary from band to band and nation to nation. Their form and content is determined by language and environment. Finally, anyone seriously undertaking the study of Indian oral traditions should be prepared to respect and preserve these traditions in their pure form. This can only be done if the written form is manipulated to conform to the rules, language, and style of Indian oral traditions. But the ultimate goal should be to achieve a balance, allowing Indian oral and written traditions to co-exist side by side without one diminishing the importance of the other.

This is a difficult task, one that can only be achieved over a long period of time. It is with this awareness that Wolfe has committed his stories to written form in the English language. His knowledge of the Saulteaux language, both in its old and new forms, is remarkable, and his oral and written mastery of the English language has made it possible for him to convey much of the meaning and richness of his oral history through the arduous task of translation. It is his goal, however, to rewrite these stories, and to write future works, in the Saulteaux language. Meanwhile, the stories as they are presented here provide a unique and insightful view into a history of a people, and an opportunity to better understand the nature and importance of the Saulteaux oral tradition and its power to preserve their language, values, and cosmology.

Harvey Knight

INTRODUCTION

From centuries past comes a path. On this path the grandfathers walked as did their grandfathers before them. Each in
his time carried the history of their people, their identity and
a way of life. Many years have passed since I heard the stories
from the grandfathers. The stories fascinated me as they were
told.

Quite often the grandfathers used a saying in the Saulteaux
language, *"Mawesha Anishnawbak Keyutotunmok."* This means, "In
times past Indian people listened."

I now know why the grandfathers felt that listening was
important. The oral tradition, in which history is embedded,
requires the use of memory. The teachings that instruct a person
in their identity, their purpose in life, their responsibility and

contribution to the well-being of others are put in the memory for safekeeping. The grandfathers wanted young people to listen, to use their minds to the utmost capacity as a storeroom. In later times, when they too became grandfathers, the stories would be passed on to the next generation, ensuring the survival of their history and way of life. As the years passed, the grandfathers passed on. Suddenly there were none. The grandfathers were gone, but not their stories.

The stories that were carefully told and retold to me when I was younger have taken on new significance for me at my age. This period in life the grandfathers called the age of reminiscence. "The age comes when the body can no longer function like it used to," they said. It is a time in which I am awake, unable to sleep, thinking of what is to become of my children and grandchildren. It is like coming to the top of a hill, turning and looking into the past from where you came, then turning into the direction of the future and viewing all its uncertainties. The mind wanders into the past, reviewing the good and the not so good, things that could have been but never were, things that were but didn't have to be. One does not reach this age merely to think of the past, but to have hope and aspirations for the future, and to do something so history and a way of life may continue for the purpose it was intended.

One grandfather told the story of an old man who lived in a camp of many wigwams by a great river. Across the river, opposite the camp, there stood on the bank a bush thick with trees. Life in the camp went on each day and the old man was a part of it. At certain times, however, the old man could be seen by the river doing something.

One day someone went over and asked him, "What are you doing here?"

"You see those trees beyond the river?" he replied, putting his work aside and seating himself. "If you look closely you will see at one place the bush is thin and beyond there is a plain. I am putting together a boat with which my children and grandchildren may cross the river. Once across the river they can make their way through the bush to the open plain beyond. I have come a long way in life. Life has been good to me. I need not cross this river; I am content to live here the rest of my life. There are many, though, particularly the young, who need to go on, through and beyond all obstacles. With my knowledge and experience, it is my duty to help them face their uncertain future. One day my tracks will come to an end and I shall go to my father and grandfathers. You will continue on this path on which we all walk."

The grandfathers realized that a time was coming when what they had to say would be important to the well-being and stability of their descendants yet to come. From predictions made before their time, they knew that in the future there would be a need for the *Anishnaybay*[1] to know of their descendency and history, their language and culture. Without this, future descendants would become lost and would be in confusion.

With ease, and never forgetting any details, the grandfathers told the stories about their family history. These stories show why certain customs are observed in a certain manner as prescribed by their cultural and spiritual tradition. In some of the stories there is humour. Another type of story told by the grandfathers and grandmothers to convey a lesson in life employed a deceiving legendary character named *Nanapusho*, who was able to communicate with all creation. He sometimes ended up a loser. Other times he did some good things and the way in which he did them was humourous. The *Nanapusho* stories, the grandfathers said, were to be told during the winter season. The stories relating to the family and the historical background of the *Anishnaybay* could be told at any season.

Each group of people, each family, has its story to tell. Some families belong to the same group and share the same story. *Akeywakeywazee* (Earth Man, also known as Earth Elder)[2], told

---

1. *Anishnaybay:* Indian, singular
   Anishnaybak: Indian, plural
2. *Akeywakeywazee* is more correctly translated as Earth Elder, coming from the notion of old man earth, but he was called Earth Man by most people.

the stories of our people. They were passed on to him by his
father, *Pinayzitt* (Partridge Foot), a man who roamed this land
before the whiteman came. His descendants now number several hundred and live in four Canadian provinces and three
American states. Each family handed down its own stories.
Other stories, belonging to other families, could not be told,
because to do so would be to steal.

Earth Elder cautioned: "There are two things in life that must
not be taken without consent. One is the family story and the
other is a song. To take these without consent is to steal." We
may say that throughout past centuries there existed in Indian
society a copyright system based on trust.

Earth Elder said, "These stories have been handed down from
father to son for how long, we don't know. The people in the
stories, *Anishnaybak,* lived as they were instructed to do. A person was responsible for himself and those around him. The
greater responsibility that lay before him each day was to his
Creator and all of creation. When he failed in this, things went
wrong and he was in sorrow." The stories that Earth Elder
and other grandfathers and grandmothers told stressed this need
to live in harmony with one another and with all creation.
That, said the Grandfather, was how the Creator of all things
wanted it to be in the beginning.

The right to tell the *Pinayzitt* family stories came to me
through my mother. Earth Man had four younger brothers.
The third in line was my mother's father *Keshickasheway mingot*
(Blessed by the Sky). According to our custom, my mother
called these uncles father and their wives mother. To me they
were grandfathers and grandmothers. Earth Man had often said
that these stories were to be told and handed down in this
family.

To be responsible for retelling the stories of the grandfathers
today, the *Anishnaybay* must renew their commitment to the
oral tradition. At the same time, we must turn to a written
tradition and use it to support, not destroy, our oral tradition.
The structure of our society in the days when the grandfathers
were still with us was very different from what we have today.

Information and instruction were transmitted to us orally, in story form, by our old people. Listening and absorbing what was told required great lengths of time. The use of the mind and memory were important; this is why the stories were told over and over again. The environment of that time held nothing to distract the listener and the storyteller. Today many things distract the listener and disrupt the storytelling. Radio, television, video, and printed material take precedence in the everyday lives of many children, and even the adults, in our present society. We are ceasing to be storytellers and listeners, and in so doing we are losing that great virtue called patience, so strongly emphasized by the grandfathers. If we are to preserve the stories that contain our history we must restore the art, practice and principles of oral storytelling. We must also commit our oral history to written form. That written form, however, must still comply with the wishes and aspirations of the grandfathers, now long gone from our numbers.

Grandfather Earth Man was well past the century mark of his life the last time I visited him. The body that was once strong and erect was now weakened and stooped with age. The eyesight that had once been so keen it could spot even the slightest movement at great distance was now diminished. The movements of a man whose life required he be quick and agile were now reduced to a shuffle. But the words that came from his mouth still flowed with ease. I could see in him what he and the other grandfathers of the past had said, "Where the body fails, the mind continues." His mind was clear and precise as he told about his days, his travels, the hardships of life and the ways of survival. He recalled the many times his people had to make crucial decisions as the changes of time engulfed them. Some changes were gradual and others took place within a short period of time. He spoke of predictions made by his elders before him and how these were being fulfilled even in his lifetime. How these would affect the children of that time, he could only entrust to the goodness and mercy of the Creator. Life and all the things necessary for a good life were given to us, he said. If they were abused and neglected, then the

Anishnaybay would cease to be what he was intended to be. The *Anishnaybay*, he concluded, is not judged by what he takes, but by what he gives. This was Grandfather as I remember him that August in 1937, a few days before I returned to boarding school. On the day I left, Grandfather Earth Man, standing outside the door of his house, spoke his last words to me. Pointing in the direction of the north he said, "*Noosis,* (grandchild) in that direction to the north, where the wind is cold, there is a Spirit that has kept me all my life in my travels. *Machan noosis* (go, grandchild), do not look back, follow the path before you, it goes far into the future."

Fifty years have passed since Grandfather spoke his words of advice and farewell to me. The accounts he gave by oral tradition are now in written form. Earth Man's stories can be put into two categories. The first three stories, as they are assembled here, lay down the principles and the concepts which provide the foundation that governed the behaviour of his people socially and spiritually in centuries past. In these stories we see why certain beliefs and customs are followed in the manner prescribed in their cultural and spiritual tradition. The rest of the stories tell of Grandfather Earth Man's experiences and those of his people, how changes affected his people socially and spiritually, how the policies that came from the agreements with the whiteman had great impact on the people of their band, and how his people regretted having settled for so little in return for so much.

When Grandfather Earth Man spoke of his days before the coming of the whiteman, he did mention chasing the noble beast, the buffalo of the Great Plains, but he rarely spoke at length about this. He told many stories about survival and many about the exploits of horse theft. The people of his band did not raise horses; they obtained them by stealing them from other Indian tribes. These tribes that they stole from lived mainly in the area to the south and to the southwest of them beyond the Missouri River. This stealing was considered an honourable achievement, worthy of mention, resulting in the wealth and prestige of the individual in their band. Since the

Pinayzitt people did not have many horses, they were unable to follow the buffalo herds as the animals migrated with the seasons. As a result, they did not depend exclusively on the buffalo to provide their food, clothing, and shelter. They hunted other animals—moose, elk, deer, bear, and waterfowl. They occasionally ventured onto the open plains to hunt the buffalo, but their survival was only partially dependent on this animal. Even after the *Peshikee* (Earth Man's Saulteaux word for the buffalo) had been exterminated by the whiteman, the Saulteaux way of life continued up to the time of the formation of the reserve system.

When the reserves were formed, there followed a period of adjustment with hardship, Earth Man said. Earth Man and his brothers settled on their new reserve in the area surrounding Goose Lake. Earth Man took a home site overlooking a valley with a lake later known as the Crooked Lake in the Qu'Appelle Valley. The twin brothers, Blessed by the Sky and Blessed by the Earth, took home sites to the west and northwest from Goose Lake. Yellow Calf took a site north of Goose Lake. The youngest member of the family, New Born Bird, did not take a home site. He left his brothers several winters later and moved to an area at the Riding Mountain in central Manitoba, and later to the Rolling River Reserve. Very little is known about this brother, only that he engaged in farming on the reserve shortly after the reserve was formed.

These were difficult times, Earth Man said. All around them the whiteman came, in numbers far greater than the Indian, and took over the land they had once hunted and gathered upon. That land was now out of bounds for them, and the hunting and gathering way of life was slowly becoming a thing of the past. The treaty agreements, made in good faith with the whiteman, were now causing a hardship for Earth Man's people. Many times they went hungry because local government people ignored their responsibilities to provide the necessities promised in the agreements. In Earth Man's story of the life and times of his brother Yellow Calf this is clearly seen. Also at this time a debate took place on personal com-

mitment to the Creator. The question was serious. Should they
or should they not honour a commitment with the whiteman,
whom they had begun to mistrust in many ways. Yellow Calf
was forced to resolve this issue and try to keep unity among
his people. This is told in the story of "The Last Raid." By
this period the name Goose Lake people was well established
as the identity of the former wandering *Pinayzitt* people. Yellow
Calf was recognized by his people as their leader, but to what
extent he was recognized by the government and church
officials of the time was unknown to Earth Man. He told of
a period of religious suppression which was held at bay for a
time by the strong personal and tribal commitment of the
Goose Lake people. The event which resulted in the banning
of all Indian religious activities is told by Standing Through
The Earth in "The Last Rain Dance."

When Earth Man told his stories, he included many facts and
reflections about his own life as a hunter. He placed strong emphasis on the sanctity of all things in creation, and how they
were given to be used in a proper and just manner. The animals
that were given for food, clothing, and shelter were not to be
wasted. Any part of these animals which was not used was to
be disposed of in an orderly manner in some clean uncon-
taminated area. The reason for this, he said, was that all animal
life is akin to the *Anishnaybay* and must not be trodden under
foot. Earth Man placed great emphasis on this; he viewed it
as a responsibility. He cautioned that, if this is not done, things
go wrong and the end result is confusion and hunger. In this
connection he often referred to the story of "Grandfather
Buffalo and the Orphan Children." This story, he said, told
what happens when the *Anishnaybay* fails in his responsibility
in life. After much suffering the Creator will give him direction
for a better life, but only if the *Anishnaybay* listens and abides
by what he is told.

In times past the grandfathers did not have a precise system
for dating events. The calendar system as we know it today
was unknown to them. It should never be said that the grandfathers' sense of time was inferior. It served their purpose in

the kind of world in which they lived. They used what they saw in creation to mark time. Plant life, in its birth, development and decay, the mating season and birth of animals, colour changes and habits of animals at certain seasons were used. Natural disasters, unusual sightings in the heavens, things that happened to them or to someone else–like death from hunger, sickness, and happenings they heard about–were used. Even their own age was used to place past events. Grandfather Earth Man said, "I was past forty winters old when we went to the valley to discuss the treaties." In recounting an event, Grandfather usually began with the season in which it occurred– like the berry season, hatching time of the fowl, or the first flight of the young birds. For an event that took place in the winter season he usually said "the mid-winter time" or "when the fog came in late winter," or "at a time when the bear cubs are born." Battles and fights between groups and individuals were also used. Usually a leader was mentioned, and where and why he fought. The details– if he won or lost–were not important, the main thing being that this event had happened. This was Grandfather's way of measuring time within a story he was telling.

Sometimes the event Grandfather used to mark time was a story in its own right. He sometimes began a story by saying, 'It was the time when Whitehead was killed within the camp and his head cut off.' The important thing here was the time when Whitehead was killed, not where he was killed or why his head was cut off. People would know that story because Whitehead is well known and that made the event very significant. It is told that Whitehead was a strange man (strange meaning that he was from a different tribe), very spiritually gifted and a daring individual. The young man with long white hair was known to have successfully led many raiding parties. His presence at any time or place was to be feared. But by this time he met his superior–someone who was more spiritually gifted and this caused his defeat. On the day of his defeat, the elder who was to defeat him made a public announcement that, at a certain time after dusk at a certain spot, a man covered with a buffalo robe would be standing. Be ready, he said, this is the feared Whitehead. At the appointed time men with concealed weapons waited at that spot. The spot was the entrance of a large lodge where a ceremony was taking place. After dusk a man covered with a buffalo robe appeared and stood at this spot. Suddenly there were great shouts as the men attacked the robe-covered man. Whitehead was killed and his head cut off. It was not known who actually killed him. The head was hung on a pole by the entrance of the lodge for all to see. He was a young man with hair that was pure white and hung down past his shoulders. In a short time this event was widely known and was used as a measurement of time. It is to be remembered that Earth Man never went into detail in telling this story because he and his people were not eye-witnesses to the event. His sole purpose in referring to the event was to establish a time when some other event occurred and begin the story that flowed from it.

In later times, after Grandfather was permanently settled on the reserve and had access to news of events from greater distances, he continued to use the dating system which he was accustomed to using. He sometimes referred to the event that occurred when the halfbreed, Aleel (Riel) had a fight (Northwest Rebellion of 1885), or that big fight which he heard was taking place across the Great Waters. According to what grandfather and other Indian people had been told, a group of people called the Boers were fighting. The only thing that Grandfather and others could relate to that sounded the same was a boar, a male pig. So the time designation was born, "the time the pig had a fight." Other events that he used were: the great fight across the Great Waters (war of 1914), and the great fever sickness that followed (flu epidemic of 1918). This was always the way that Grandfather measured time, because these were significant events that happened in his lifetime.

Grandfather Earth Man observed many changes during his lifetime, which spanned more than a century. His life began at a time when the land was still open and provided the daily necessities of everyday life. This land, in centuries past, was the *Anishnaybay* inheritance. From it came his source of well-being and belonging. From this same source comes the historical path that is recorded in this oral history of the *Pinayzitt* family.

"I tell you this so you will know and remember." These words were spoken by *Kakeymawnokay* (Makes it Rain), the last surviving grandson of *Pinayzitt,* before his footprints came to an end. *Kakeymawnokay,* also known as Young Boy Sanquis, gave this message to his son when he finished recounting for the last time the stories and history of his fathers and grandfathers. This was a direct instruction to my generation to assume the responsibility of preserving our family's history for the grandchildren and the children yet to come.

These same stories were told to me when I was a young boy by my grandfather, *Akeywakeywazee* (Earth Elder). I clearly remember the times I stayed with Earth Elder when I was home from residential school. During those winter evenings I and several of his other grandsons would give him some tobacco and he would tell us stories in his small lamplit house near the warmth of the wood stove. He usually told the same stories over and over again, but each time he added new life to them. So they were never boring. Now, many years later, these stories are being recalled to my memory in all their rich visual and meaningful detail, for now I've become a grandfather too and my responsibility to carry on the history of my people has only begun.

It took a number of years of thinking before I could assume this responsibility, for many things had to be considered. I pondered the purpose of oral tradition. I knew it was used by the grandfathers to preserve a way of life through remembering the stories which make up not only the history of a family but the history of a nation. The stories are very important because they contain a philosophy of life that is adaptable to any time and any place. The prime responsibility of the storyteller or oral historian, therefore, is to ensure that the stories are preserved intact and unaltered. To take out or add content to these stories destroys the truth found therein.

It is important to note that these stories are best told in the original Saulteaux language. The language is a vital element of the oral tradition for it conveys the full picture, the meaning and the feelings of the story. It is very difficult to translate some of the old Saulteaux terms into English.

Before fulfilling this elder's request I also had to consider whether it was possible to bring the oral tradition together with the written tradition. I concluded that the two could co-exist as long as one doesn't try to diminish the importance of either one. The stories must continue to be told in oral form, and members of our Indian society must be trained in this manner. In this respect it is important to stay within the boundaries of the principles and rules that govern oral tradition when transmitting the stories in written form. In so doing we are mindful that the oral tradition is and will continue to be a vital aspect of Indian culture and society. In this work, then, I have endeavored to utilize both traditions to bring forth the Saulteaux oral history of the *Pinayzitt* family.

ACKNOWLEDGEMENTS

I am deeply indebted to the following:

Akeywakeywazee (Earth Elder)
My grandfather for his stories and advice

Shapakomicappow (Standing Through the Earth)
My grandfather for his stories and advice

Osowwacekak (Hilda Pelltier)
My aunt and one of the two surviving granddaughters of Pinayzitt for the names of the old people and her moral support.

Sakaywayaniqadok (Jean Gayewish)
Of the Rolling River Band, Manitoba, one of two surviving granddaughters of Pinayzitt, for contribution and verification of genealogy list.

My thanks also to the great grandchildren of *Pinayzitt* who have given their support and information:

Albert Moses Sanquis, Sakimay Band, Saskatchewan.

Margret Huntinghawk Mckay, Waywaysecappo Band, Manitoba.

Liza Iron Bear Henry, Turtle Mountains Chippawa Tribe, North Dakota.

My gratitude to my son Jonathan who listened to the stories and drew the map.

My sincere thanks to these for their efforts and encouragements in bring this book to reality:

Caroline Heath
Of Fifth House Publishers, Saskatoon for editing the final draft of the manuscript and for the work and financial investment in publishing and promoting the book.

Harvey Knight
Of Saskatoon for editing the first draft of the manuscript and for his moral and consultative support. In return I have given and continue to give Harvey knowledge towards his personal goals in the field of oral traditions.

Diane Knight
Of the same city for typing and proofreading the first draft and for her moral support. In return I have given her a story in the manner of oral tradition principles.

Wil Campbell
Of The Gabriel Crossing Foundation for the moral, financial, and continuing promotional support. In return I have committed my support in his endeavors.

Maria Campbell
Of The Gabriel Crossing Foundation for her support, advice and contribution to the development of the book.

Alexander Wolfe
Saskatoon, Saskatchewan
November 23,1987

THE SOUND OF DANCING

told by Earth Elder, retold by Standing Through the Earth

Many years ago when Indians roamed this land, hunting and gathering for their survival, it was not uncommon for small groups to fall victim to raiding parties of hostile Indians of other tribes. The following account is of one little boy who survived to tell the tale of what happened to his people.

The camp was small. It was winter when the attack came. So ferocious that there was no hope of survival. The grandfather, covered only with a buffalo robe, fled with his grandson in hand. Their flight was short-lived as the grandfather was soon struck down by blows. In a last attempt to save his grandson, he grabbed him and threw himself on top of the boy, covering both of them with his buffalo robe.

As time went by everything became quiet.

1

The boy asked his grandfather, "How long will we be here?" The grandfather answered, "I will try to keep you as long as I can." With this the boy fell asleep lying under the robe with his grandfather. In time the boy awoke. He could hear his grandfather talking with people, as if they were visiting. He wondered who they were, but did not dare ask his grandfather, because he knew that when older people were speaking it was impolite to interrupt. One was supposed to listen and learn from what they spoke about. Again, he fell back to sleep. At times when the boy awoke all would be quiet, as if it were night, and again he would keep silent lest he waken Grandfather, who was asleep. It was at these quiet times that he could hear in the distance the sounds of a drum with people singing, the sounds of people as they danced, and people speaking in remembrance of those gone before them. All this puzzled the boy, and at times when he awoke and Grandfather was awake he longed to ask him, but always Grandfather was talking to someone else.

After some time had gone by, the boy awoke again and all was quiet. He wondered, was it really nighttime? Why was it so quiet? Without disturbing Grandfather the boy slowly lifted the buffalo robe, just a tiny bit and peeked out. It was daylight. As the boy lay beside Grandfather he wondered what was happening to him and the place where they were. Again he heard Grandfather awaken and begin talking to the others as he always did. The boy waited for the right time to speak, to ask Grandfather why there were times of quiet, why he heard in the distance people singing and speaking of those who were no longer with them. Why all these things? Even now Grandfather was speaking to someone, as if he was visiting. Yet he never left. How long was he to lie here beside his grandfather. Grandfather had said, "I will try to keep you as long as I can."

When the right time came and Grandfather was silent for a moment the boy spoke, "Grandfather, why is it there are times when everything is quiet and in the distance I hear people. Then at other times you seem awake, you talk to others as if you were visiting. Why all these things, and how long are we to be here?"

Grandfather spoke, "My grandson, the time has come for you to go. I have kept my promise for I have kept you as long as I could. Now you must leave. But first I will speak of the things you ask. When my day ends, your day begins. With that you must leave. When it is quiet it is my night, and I must begin to prepare for my next day, just as you must be quiet in your night and rest for your next day. Those that you hear in the distance are your people; they are in their day. It is their time to sing and dance, to remember those of us who are no longer there, to remember what we had to say about life and how it should be lived. You must tell all that I tell you to your people – to those who will accept your word, and even to those who will doubt you. You must remember how to use those things that are yours and to share with others, even with us who are here. The times when I speak to others here are during my day. There are many who are here. We also have our song and dance, and in time to come you will be here. For this reason your tears shall not flow when you leave here at the end of my day to begin your day. When you leave here you will go due south. After you have made four camps you will reach your people. Go, my grandson, it is time to begin your day and tell all that I have told you.

With this the boy lifted the buffalo robe which covered him and his grandfather. It was daylight. Spring had come. The snow had melted on the hills. Only the bushes and the low spots had snow. Gently he covered Grandfather, whom he now knew had been gone for many days. Grandfather's spirit had kept him warm and alive. As he looked at the remains of those who had fallen in the attack, he felt a lump in his throat, but Grandfather had said that no tears should flow. He knew if he cried Grandfather would hear. Slowly the boy began to walk, his face to the south. When evening came he made camp. In the quiet of the evening the boy remembered all that Grandfather had said. To the north the northern lights danced. He remembered grandfather's words: we also have our song and dance. On the morning of the fourth camp, as the boy walked along, he smelled wood smoke and, going further over a ridge, he sighted a camp. He had found his people.

When the boy told what his grandfather had said and how he had survived, there were some who questioned his story and demanded to see the place where the attack had taken place during the past winter. In this the boy saw Grandfather's words coming true because he had said there would be those who did not accept his story of survival. In due time the boy led a group of men to the site. There they found the remains of those who had died in the attack. Grandfather still lay there covered with the buffalo robe as the grandson had left him.

THE ORPHAN CHILDREN

told by Earth Elder, retold by Standing Through the Earth

In days gone by when Indian people lived in this land in accordance with the laws of nature, and spiritual direction was necessary for survival, the Creator showed love and mercy to the unfortunate and the poor. That compassion shaped the lives of a little boy and his sister who had been orphaned and were being raised by relatives.

Life was not easy for these children, even though tribal custom and law directed their relatives to provide and care for them. Often times they were hungry, and it was at these times that the little boy would take his little sister, and, wandering into the surrounding area, they would feed on berries and the roots of plants that grew there. The relatives never missed them as they wandered about each day eating whatever they found, returning only in the evening to sleep. As their food supply diminished they wandered further and further away.

One day as the little boy and his sister walked hand in hand in search of food the boy asked, "Should we leave this place? There is much food to be found elsewhere. I would look after you, and we would be full and never have to come back to this place."

The little girl, not really understanding the true nature of the question, answered yes. As they wandered further and further they found more berries and roots of plants to eat. They were satisfied. When night came they made camp and in the morning they continued, eating what food they found. This went on for several days and then one day they came upon a small deserted colt. As children will do, they went over to the colt and began petting it. The colt was friendly and did not run away.

The boy said, "We will take the colt as our own. You, little sister, will ride it."

During the days that followed, the children and the colt played, searched for food, and became accustomed to the ways of survival. When the children made camp the colt was always near. When they travelled the little girl rode the colt.

It was on one of these days of travel that an incident happened that would change their lives. Suddenly, in front of them on a hill, they spotted a man on a horse watching them. He wore a feather hat and was dressed in buckskin. Unknown to the children, he was the chief of a band of Indians who lived to the west. As the chief watched the two children and the colt, he was joined by other mounted members of his party. He felt compassion for the children and ordered that they be brought to him. When this was done he announced that he would adopt the children and raise them as his own. When the party returned to camp the children were brought into the chief's wigwam and there they lived.

As the boy grew older and stronger he accompanied his adopted father on hunts, learning the habits and ways of all the animals and the signs in nature as they related to survival.

He grew to be a wise young man, knowledgeable in spiritual matters and skillful as a hunter, and a very handsome young man. The little girl in the meantime also grew and became very beautiful. Under the guidance of the chief's wife, she also became adept at tanning, sewing and other skills, all of which were considered the makings of a good and honest mother and wife. Their colt also grew to be a beautiful horse. The girl often rode it, and she became an excellent rider. Both of the children, from the time they arrived and while they were growing up, were dearly loved by the chief and his wife and their family.

This chief often gathered his family together and told them of happenings in the past and events that were to occur in the future. It was at one of these family gatherings that he told his adopted son and daughter that they did not belong at his wigwam, that they belonged to another world, another people.

The chief said, "I felt compassion toward you because you were alone, without a family and a wigwam where you would learn how to use the things of life. You must now return to your own, to teach and lead your people. Your people have suffered greatly since you left; they are now scattered. When you find them they will be afraid of you, but in time they will come to know and trust you. You both shall show and teach them what you have learned and in that way they will become a strong and caring people. I will give you a horse and provide the necessary things for your journey. You will travel from here to the east and after many days you will see your people. They will be afraid and run from you, but you will overcome their fear. In time to come, when you are in need, you will ride your horse to the west, singing the song I will give you. My children will hear you and will follow you to a place you will choose. In this way they will meet your needs. I have spoken. I am Grandfather Buffalo."

After much preparation the young man and his sister left, he on the horse given to him by the chief, and she on the horse they had found as a colt when they were children. During the many days of their travel they spoke and wondered many times about their adopted father and his family. Little by little they realized, from the wisdom that had been spoken to them and the future foretold, that they had entered into and lived in a world of spirituality. Now they were returning to their own world.

One day as they were travelling they spotted some Indians, who upon seeing them, ran for cover into a patch of woods. The boy and girl stopped riding. After a long wait they saw a woman appear and slowly approach them. The young man spoke to her. He asked where the rest were and in what direction their camp lay. The woman hesitated for a while and then slowly pointed to the east.

She then asked, "Who are you?"

The young man answered, "I am the orphan boy and this is my little sister. We left and now we have come back to be with our people."

Hesitantly the woman came near. She looked into the face of the young man and then withdrew.

"It cannot be," the woman said, "but in your face I see the face of my brother who left us many winters ago. I took his children – a boy and a girl – but lost them. All these years I have searched, but found no trace of them."

In his mind the young man could still see himself as a boy leading his sister by the hand in search of berries and roots to eat. He remembered the days and nights of hunger, their journey to the wigwam of Grandfather Buffalo. He also remembered the wisdom and concern Grandfather Buffalo had for them, the things he had taught him, and why he sent him and his sister back to teach and gather his scattered people. He now stood before one of those people, his aunt, whom he vaguely remembered and knew nothing about.

Turning to his sister he asked, "Do you know anything about the time when we were little?"

The girl answered, "No."

Turning to the woman he said, "We are the children that you lost, we have come back to be with you and the rest of our people."

After greetings, the woman led the young couple to what

was left of their people. The past winters had been hard on them and many had passed on due to starvation and sickness. After looking over the condition of the people the young man knew their needs were many, but he knew Grandfather Buffalo could provide for them. A day's journey to the west he had noted a cliff, and he knew that this was where he would lead the children of Grandfather Buffalo. He would use the song and prayer ritual that Grandfather Buffalo had given him. Taking a number of men they left for this area. When they neared the site he instructed the men to wait below the cliff. He rode in a circle, singing the song Grandfather Buffalo had given him. During his ride he was joined by a young male yearling buffalo followed by five more buffalo. The animals followed him as he rode in the direction of the cliff. When he came to the edge of the precipice, he swung his horse to the side, letting the animals fall to their deaths at the bottom of the cliff, where the waiting men slaughtered them.

The young man and his sister instructed their people carefully. The people of his camp prospered, gained strength physically, spiritually, and in numbers. Both the young man and his sister took mates from among their people and had children. They both lived to a ripe old age, instructing and caring for their people, for this was why Grandfather Buffalo had taken them, to instruct them in the ways that Indians were to live, to be a strong and caring people.

GRANDFATHER BEAR
told by Earth Elder

Many years ago, when Indians lived in close harmony with nature and spiritual beliefs were the basis of everyday life, there lived in a certain camp a girl and a boy of very different standing. The girl was the daughter of a local chief, lovely and the only child. The boy was an orphan, poor but handsome, who lived with relatives. Unknown to the chief and the boy's relatives, this boy and girl loved each other. They dared not make their feeling public, however, because of their different backgrounds and upbringing. Tribal customs prevented them from seeing each other in public or formally announcing their love and their desire to commit themselves to one another. The girl was a member of the chief's family, a family held in high esteem. For a young unmarried female to be seen in the company of an unmarried male was considered improper. The boy's

11

poverty added to the difficulty. In those days when a male desired a maiden's hand in marriage, custom demanded that he approach the father of his intended with gifts for the father's blessing and approval. The number of horses owned by the individual indicated a level of wealth, hence prestige. The orphan boy owned no horses. These customs and his status prevented the orphan boy from showing his true intentions. After all, who was he but an *opeenesash* (one with nothing) and the girl knew this. What were they to do?

Our people in those days did not raise horses. Instead, they stole from other tribes who owned them, often killing to obtain them. This was done by committing one's self to the perils and dangers of the raid, by going into hostile territory to steal and bring back the prize which was the horse. Only the brave dared to take such a risk, only the strong and the spiritually-oriented dared to go. Such were the qualities of men who went on raiding ventures and into battles. To go and to return meant wealth and prestige.

As the two young people pondered in their hearts their secret commitment to each other, there went out an announcement in their camp. A certain man had committed himself to lead a party of men beyond the Snow Mountains for the purpose of obtaining horses. An invitation was extended to all males willing to face possible death for the reward of horse ownership. Each male committed to making the journey was to make preparations, in moccasins and supplies, and be ready in early spring when the south winds blew and the creeks began to flow.

When spring came the men gathered together on the eve of their departure to make their final vows in song and prayer. Among them was the orphan boy, for he too was determined to challenge the unknown. The chief's daughter had secretly made his moccasins and rawhide ropes in the hope that he would bring back the horses necessary for their commitment to each other. At dawn the party left, the leader in front and the orphan boy in the rear, because he was the youngest of the party. Each man was told to always look forward in the direction they were going. If any man looked back, he was sent back to his wigwam to put on his wife's dress as a sign that he was not a man.

Many days passed as the party journeyed, always on the lookout for any signs of movement. As they walked, the orphan boy's mind wandered into the past and into the future. From the past he recalled the birds and animals he had seen and heard, the maiden who waited for him and the many times hunger and thirst had been his companions. The future made itself known to him by the company of the men with whom he travelled. They shared with him their food, words of comfort, and hope. Finally, in early summer, they sighted the Snow Mountains in the distance. The mountain tops shone like mirrors in the sunlight. Beyond these mountains lay the land of strange and hostile Indians who had many horses. Each day brought the mountains closer and finally one day the party stood before a great forest at the base of the Snow Mountains. Entering the forest they made camp and settled down.

The leader spoke, "Beyond these mountains I have been given many horses, which some of you will bring back. Some of you will not return to the land from where we came. At dawn two scouts will leave and in four days they will return with news of where the horses are and the numbers of those who camp there with the horses."

Three days went by and while the men of the party were waiting they told each other why they were there at this time. Some told of visions and dreams which had given them the courage and stability to face the many challenges they had encountered in life. The orphan boy listened and hoped that he too would be blessed with the courage to overcome this, his first challenge. Could it be that on the other side of these mountains he would reach his final resting place, where in time his body would become part of the green grass and this beautiful earth?

Towards the end of the third day, the scouts returned with the news, "Beyond these moutains there is a small creek flowing from a canyon. At the head of this canyon there is a camp, not large, and in the back of this canyon a large herd of horses is kept." Hearing this the leader gave thanks for in locating the horses he had already overcome his challenge. Now it was up to each man to overcome his own. They would make the raid at dawn of the the fourth day. After hearing the scouts' report, the men of the party continued and on the eve of the third day they surveyed the camp to determine the number of men in camp and the number who guarded the horses in the canyon. When night came, the men lay down, not to sleep but to watch the movement of the camp and the horses. The orphan boy lay down to rest, but he could not sleep. His thoughts were of his father, his mother and grandfather. He had hardly known these people for they had passed on when he was small. In the years of hardship when he was growing up, the boy had at times felt the presence of his grandfather, as if he were near. He felt that presence again. This feeling gave him courage and hope. The orphan knew he was no longer a boy but a man ready to meet his challenge. For this he was thankful.

During the night the orphan boy fell asleep and as he slept Grandfather came to him and said, "I am Grandfather. To you, grandson, I give two horses – one white and one black – but to receive them you must know the meaning of pain."

When the orphan boy awoke, it was nearly dawn and the party was beginning to move toward the herd of horses in the canyon. At a signal from the leader the raid was on. The orphan boy, his rawhide rope in hand, managed to catch a horse, but while trying to catch a second horse, a white one, he was struck in the thigh and knee with arrows which tore his flesh. He managed to catch the horse and mount it in spite of his wounds. Riding the white horse and leading the other, the orphan boy joined the other men who were heading into the mountains, pursued by the men from the camp. Following a planned escape route the raiding party rode as fast as the horses would travel. They fled through the mountains until at last, the horses being winded and slowing down, they stopped to count how many men they had lost and how many horses they had captured.

The orphan boy made it this far and then fell from his horse, exhausted from the loss of blood. His wounds were so great that his blood was splattered on the rump and side of the white horse he was riding. The flight continued at a slower pace due to the orphan boy's wounds and by morning they had reached the forest on the other side of the mountains.

Here they stopped to rest and treat their wounds. The orphan boy realised that his wounds were serious and urged the men to build a wigwam for him, to stock it with meat, water and wood, and leave him there. He did not think he would survive the return trip and he feared that his condition would only slow the party down. He also told the men that he had met his challenge and obtained what he wanted, meaning the two horses. He instructed one of the men to take his horses to the chief's daughter, since it was for her that he had challenged the unknown. The men erected a large wigwam and stocked it as the orphan boy had requested. Before leaving, they gave him many arrows to defend himself if he was attacked.

Summer passed and the leaves on the trees began to show their colours. Every day the chief's daughter scanned the horizon for movement, for she knew the men would soon return. Suddenly one day there were shouts in the camp. A group of riders and horses had been sighted on a ridge in the distance. One of the group had been riding back and forth to show they were friendly. This caused great excitement in the camp, and people prepared to welcome their returning men. As the party neared the camp the men from the party shouted the names of those who had not returned, saying they were men. The chief's daughter waited and listened, hoping the orphan boy's name would not be called out. Then she heard his name and shouts saying he was a man. From this she knew the orphan boy had not returned. The sounds of singing filled the camp as a victory dance began. Tearfully the girl withdrew into her father's wigwam. She untied her braids and let her hair down as a sign of mourning. As she was thus beginning her mourning, a call came from outside the wigwam. A man from the raiding party wished to speak to her. When she stepped outside there stood a man holding two horses, one white and the other black. He told her that the orphan boy had not been killed and these two horses were to be hers. It was the orphan boy's wish. The man told how the orphan boy had been seriously wounded and at his request had been left in a wigwam in a forest at the base of the Snow Mountains. That had been in summer and it was now the fall season. Maybe he was still alive. The girl asked the man to describe the area – the mountain peaks, rivers and the valleys. After obtaining as much information as she could, the girl withdrew into her father's wigwam to make preparation for a journey to find the orphan boy. She made a bundle of four pairs of moccasins and enough dried meat to last the journey. While the singing and victory dance were still going on, she kissed her mother and father goodbye, explaining to them that she had to go and find the orphan boy and bring him back.

Soon the girl could no longer hear the victory dance as she ran toward her destination. She ran day and night, stopping only to eat and change her moccasins as they wore out. She ran many days and nights until, finally, one day she sighted the tops of the Snow Mountains shining in the distance. The next morning she began to look for the landmarks that had been described to her. As she neared the mountains she recognized the landmarks and made for them. There at the base of the mountain was the forest. Making her way into the forest she soon caught the scent of woodsmoke, and going deeper into the forest she came upon a large wigwam. All was quiet. She did not know what to expect.

As she neared the door of the wigwam, a voice came from within, "If you must kill me I will take many of you with me."

The orphan boy had heard the steps. Knowing they were not animal but human, he had prepared by placing all the arrows beside him and one in his bow which he aimed toward the door.

Realizing the danger she was in, she called him by name and asked is he was all right.

He answered, "Yes."

The girl opened the door and went in. There sat the orphan boy. He was thin. His untreated wounds made it difficult for him to move. His food supply was nearly gone. His supply of wood was low. The hides for holding water, which had been fastened to stakes driven into the ground, were nearly dry. Since the departure of the raiding party the orphan boy had only eaten, drunk and made fire to keep alive. The girl immediately set about building a fire, getting fresh water, and feeding him. Then she went into the forest to gather herbs and cleaned and dressed his wounds. After that she spent her days gathering and hunting for it was now late in the fall season and they would need food for the long winter. The young couple lived in comfort that winter because she became a skillful hunter and he was recovering from his wounds under her care. During the long winter evenings he told her of his experiences with the raiding party. And many times during the long days and nights he thought about the past and wondered what the future would hold, what their future would be like if he failed in his commitment, what it held if he succeeded. The other question returned to him often, too, was he alone or was he not? He told of his grandfather's presence and what it meant to him, told how Grandfather had spoken to him in a dream saying, "Grandson, I give to you two horses, but to receive them you must know the meaning of pain." He remembered how lonely and abandoned he had felt after the men of the party left. Now he was happy and thankful for her presence.

She likewise spoke of waiting for this return, of her journey and of how her life had now been turned from sorrow to happiness.

Days went by and soon warm winds began to blow from the south, causing the snow to thaw. Early one morning he told her that Grandfather had come to him in a dream last night and said, "It is now time for you to leave and go to your people. I have had my rest. You must be ready to leave when I come."

The orphan boy instructed her to prepare a bundle of food for four days' journey and four pairs of moccasins for herself as she would need them. Having done this they waited for Grandfather's arrival.

Each evening a light fog settled in the forest, lasting all night and well past sunrise and into the morning of the next day. This the orphan boy took to be a signal that grandfather would soon be arriving. At dusk one evening the young couple heard a roar outside their door, not loud but distinct. This was Grandfather's signal that he was there. Taking their bundle, the young couple opened the door, and stepping out, they saw a huge black bear. The orphan boy said to the girl, "This is Grandfather. He will take us back to our people. I will ride him with the bundle and you will run beside him." With orphan boy on his back, the bear started at a slow pace and gradually gained speed, the girl running beside him. The bear and the girl ran all night and at dawn the bear stopped.

The orphan boy got off and said, "We will make camp here and when Grandfather has had his rest he will be back."

The young couple ate, and rested for the remainder of the day. The girl changed her moccasins as she had worn out a pair in the all-night run. At dusk the bear appeared again and the same thing happened. The bear and girl ran all night, stopping at dawn to make camp and rest.

This happened for two more nights and at dawn of the fourth night's run the orphan boy got off the bear and said, "This is as far as Grandfather can take us. From here we must walk. Before this day is over we will see our people."

With this the bear turned and walked in the direction from which he had come and the young couple walked on.

Walking was difficult for the orphan boy, for although his wounded leg had healed, it had stiffened, causing him to walk with a limp. Past midday they came to a ridge and, reaching the top, they sighted a camp in the distance. The orphan boy instructed the girl to run back and forth to signify that they were friendly. They were sighted almost immediately in camp and riders were sent out to meet and identify them.

When they were recognized, a rider was sent back to camp to tell the chief that his daughter had returned. During the winter season the chief and his wife, thinking that they had lost their only child, had gone into a period of mourning and for this reason they were rarely seen outside their wigwam. When the riders brought them the news of the approaching pair, they were overjoyed. As the orphan boy, no longer a boy but a man, and the chief's daughter approached the chief's wigwam, the chief and his wife came out. After many tearful kisses the chief returned to his wigwam. He came out bearing his eagle feather hat. After assembling his people he announced, "This day I have been blessed. My only child, a daughter, has returned and with her I have gained a son."

Placing the feather hat on the orphan boy's head he declared, "He is now your chief."

And so it was.

MY FIRST GUN
told by Earth Elder

On the wall of grandfather Earth Elder's small house hung two guns. One was old with a tied-up stock, the other was a newer one. The old gun was the one that had accompanied grandfather Earth Elder during the days of uncertainty, when his body was racked with the dread disease called smallpox. My mother told me that after grandfather Earth Elder passed on in December of 1937 the local farm instructor, Tom Guest, asked the family for the guns. He said he wanted them as a reminder of his good friendship with Earth Man. They were given to him. In later years Tom Guest, then retired, was asked about the guns. His response was that he had donated them to a museum. Wherever those guns hang today–viewed by many–lies a story that records a crucial event in Earth Elder's life and in our history. This is the story as told by Earth Elder.

From our ancestral home at *Otaominsacagun* (Strawberry Lake) our fathers made journeys west to a camp situated on the eastern slopes of the Cypress Hills. This is where another band of Saulteaux, along with some Cree, made their ancestral home. Our fathers went there to visit and to hunt. In later years the younger of my twin brothers, *Akeyashewaymingot,* took a wife from this band.

In those earlier times prairie fires sometimes swept the land, forcing all the game to flee. After a fire went through there would be nothing left, no plants, no animals, only burnt ground as far as the eye could see. We survived the fires by going to any place where there was water. This is why the area around Strawberry Lake was our home. In times of fire we would go into the water. From the high ground around the lake we could see a long way to the south and to the west. On this high ground there were always some men who watched for any movement on the horizon.

Our fathers periodically journeyed south to the hill country, where *Assincaocepeeod* (rock with written symbols) is found.[1] There they would fast and pray. They believed that the symbols on the rock at this spot described the level on which the Indian was placed, at the time of creation, a level that defined his responsibility and role in future times.

There were times when no buffalo were to be found in the area around Strawberry Lake. In hunger our people would go south to the small river called *Peecoshecepee* (Sandfly River). Following the river downstream in a southeasterly direction and then going across the prairie they would reach a hill called *Peshekeykatat* (Buffalo Lodge, west of Towner, N.D.). This was one of the places where Grandfather Buffalo was to be found. When the *Anishnaybak* approached the hill in humility and in a proper frame of mind, Grandfather Buffalo could be seen grazing on the hilltop. This meant other buffalo would be found in the immediate area – not many but enough to meet the needs

---

1. Now called Writing Rock, situated south of Altona, North Dakota.

of those who came. There were some foolish Indians who desired the buffalo who grazed on the hilltop. When they reached the hilltop, they found nothing. The other buffalo who were usually found in the area after a sighting of Grandfather Buffalo would also be gone. These Indians would leave empty-handed and hungry.

Indians from other tribes also came to this hill in search of buffalo. There was never any trouble – no fighting or stealing – among those who came for food. There are many stories about this hill and the area around it. I know some of them, but I could not tell them. These stories belong to other families.

Our people also roamed and hunted to the east as far as the place where the two big rivers, the Qu'Appelle and Assiniboine, meet and go together and continue in an easterly direction.

To the north, we hunted and roamed only on the south side of *Owaycepee* (This River, referring to the Qu'Appelle River). It seems that the Qu'appelle River had no specific name as did the lakes – Crooked and Round Lakes. Very seldom did we venture north beyond This River.

During these wanderings, our people heard from other Indians whom they met that there was a store by the Red Water River (Red River) that had many goods to trade. This interested me and others. My father had a gun. Where he got it from I don't know. On my hunting trips I sometimes used this gun. This made me want to have a gun of my own. The old way of hunting with the bow and arrow was all right, but sometimes the wait for the game was long. With the gun it is easier to kill the game, because you don't have to get so close to the animal, but the noise frightens other animals. I have killed many small animals with a club, including beaver. A beaver will sleep on a riverbank in early spring after it has finished feeding, and you can sneak up on him. In this way I hunted several winter and spring seasons to collect enough *atawagun* (animal fur to sell) to buy the things I wanted for my hunting trips. Finally I had collected enough to make the trip to the store at the Red Water River.

It was early summer when we left to make the journey to the store. There were about twenty of us. Our leader was an older man who knew the way. We did not travel very fast because our packs were heavy. By late summer we arrived at the great camp where the store was. I had never seen so many big houses. The store, too, was big and had many goods for trade. When I traded my fur, I bought a gun, a knife, and a copper pail. The others bought things like yard goods, mirrors, beads and blankets. Some bought tea and tobacco, which were considered items of great value. After a few days' rest and looking around, we began the journey home.

Several days into the journey, one of the men complained of aches and pains in his body. A severe fever hit him and he developed a rash on his arms and legs. The rash turned into pimples. The man lived only another day and a night and then he was gone. Before the man went he instucted that his belongings should be taken back to his family. In the days that followed other men fell sick in the same way and passed on. In desperation we sought amongst our numbers for someone who could seek a vision as to why this was happening to us. There was such a man in our midst. In the evening after we made camp, the man sang and prayed and had a vision. When he was finished, he made an announcement to the group. In the vision he had been told that a strange sickness brought to this land by the whiteman would kill us all except for one man. And that person would survive with aid from an animal. The vision directed that, from now on, when a man passed on, everything he owned should be left behind. Using anything that belonged to a person who had this strange sickness would pass the sickness to the next person. We were told to keep a certain distance from each other, to prevent the sickness from spreading.

Each passing day saw our numbers get smaller. Finally, we were only a few. We were not far from home, but the distance we covered each day became shorter and shorter as our men grew weaker. One night as I slept an animal came to me and said, "Many more winters will pass in your life if you do what

I will tell you. The scent that I carry will save you and the fat from my body will heal you." The animal who spoke to me was a skunk. In the morning we continued our journey, but by noonday my companions could go no further, as they had come down with a fever. I too began to ache in the legs and in the arms. The fever was coming upon me. My only hope was to search and find the animal who had promised to help me. I began my search. As I walked there was a rustle in some tall grass beside me. Turning, peering into the tall grass, I saw there in front of me a big skunk. I killed the skunk and in a short time had it butchered. I saved the bladder and its contents, pouring the fluid from the skunk's bladder into my pail and adding some water. I drank my medicine. The taste was very bitter. Returning to my companions, I found them in a coma with a high fever. All night I sat with them, pouring in their mouths small amounts of the medicine that I had made from the fluid taken from the skunk's bladder. The next day one man passed on. The others regained consciousness and lived another day. But my medicine had come to them too late. I was now alone and could feel the strange sickness coming upon me. I decided to travel as far as possible while I could. Good fortune was with me. I managed to kill another skunk and I found a sheltered spot by a small lake, where I decided to stay. In the days that followed pimples appeared on my arms and legs and on the rest of my body. When these pimples broke they became little scabs. I rendered the fat from the skunk and applied it to the scabs. I was in constant pain. For many days, I don't know how many, this sickness continued. The fever finally left me, but the scabs continued to be sore. With the fall season coming I knew I must find a better spot for the winter. To find my people would not be good, for I knew my sickness would hurt them. With each passing day I felt better. So I went about building a wigwam in a place that had plenty of trees and wood. Every day I drank a little of the medicine that I had made. That winter I did not have any colds. This was good, because I needed all my strength to recover from the smallpox and to look after my needs. By spring all the scabs on my body had healed, leaving pock marks where the scabs had been. I was grateful; I had survived the strange sickness that killed off all my companions.

It was not till early in the summer season that I made contact with my people. When I did, I warned them to stay at a distance from me. This they did. When they wished to tell me something they would shout to me from a distance, and I would shout back. To visit meant a lot of shouting. If something was to be given to me my people would leave it at a distance, and when they left, I would go and get it. For three summer and two winter seasons I lived alone, usually a short distance from the camp. When my father passed on I joined my people in their camp and they did not get the strange sickness from me.

When Earth Elder had finished his story, he unbuttoned his shirt and there on his chest were the pock marks. Then he pulled up the sleeves of his shirt and the marks were there also. He said that during the winter in 1919, when so many people in this land lost their lives in the flu epidemic, not one member of Earth Elder's band died. This was because the medicine made from the liquid found in the skunk's bladder was used in every home throughout that entire winter. This same medicine that had saved Earth Elder was to save his people from another sickness many years later.

PREDICTIONS
told by Earth Elder

This story, told by Grandfather Earth Elder, deals with the subject of predictions. Grandfather stressed that predictions have an important role in the Indian way of life. Many years before his time—even before his father's time—there were among the Indian people certain men and women who were blessed with special gifts. Some had the gift of prophecy. From these people came the prediction of events that were to occur. The predictions described what people would do, where these events would take place, and in many cases, why they would happen. Through these predictions the Anishnaybay was aware of the changes to come.

One of these predictions told of the coming of the whiteman—of how he would come and what he would do. Other predictions told that there would be much confusion among Indian people after the arrival of the whiteman. The confusion, which would be caused by the introduction of habits and ways of an alien culture, would lead to a loss of identity and

27

a neglect of the ways of respect. After the whiteman comes, said the predictions, the Indian will look like an Indian, but he will not know the ways given to him by his Creator—the ways that teach him to be a caring and sharing person. Having this knowledge the Anishnaybay waited for the coming of the whiteman. Some waited in fear, some saw it as challenge, and others a curiousity.

When this story took place, Earth Elder's people had already seen many whitemen. They first encountered the whiteman on their way to Goose Lake, where they went to hunt geese. To get to the lake, the band had to cross the Fort Ellice trail which ran from Fort Garry in the east to Fort Qu'Appelle in the west. (Parts of this trail are still visible today on the southern edge of the Sakimay reserve in Saskatchewan.) The *Anishnaybay* was not too concerned about these whitemen, who were hauling their goods in two-wheeled carts on this trail, because predictions said this would happen. Their concern was what the whiteman would do after great numbers of them had arrived on Indian land. Prediction said the whiteman's numbers would eventually cover the entire land. This to Earth Elder's people was frightening.

At this time the *Anishnaybak* were a leaderless people. *Pinayzitt*, hereditary chief of the band, had already passed on. During his sickness with the smallpox Earth Elder was not able to serve as chief, and even after that he declined the position. His younger brother, *Osowapeshkez* (Yellow Calf), acted as leader and chief at times. Yellow Calf was an outspoken man with radical attitudes. This lead to his downfall as chief in later years. As long as the *Anishnaybak* had no leader, all decisions about where and when to move rested with the whole band. At this time there were rumours of greater and more frightening things to come. One of these was to be the building of the railroad. The predictions spoke of an iron road on which would travel something that looked like a great worm. It would contain fire, make much noise and blow clouds of smoke into the sky. In this would ride the whiteman in great numbers.

It was early summer when Earth Elder's people moved from the west and camped on a ridge overlooking the prairies to the east. The site overlooks the present town of Grenfell in Saskatchewan.

One day a small dark cloud of smoke was seen on the horizon to the east. At first the sighting caused no excitement in the camp. Probably a fire of some sort, they thought. A few days went by and the smoke was still there. Now there began to be some concern among the people. Two men were chosen as scouts, and were sent to investigate what and how large the fire was. In two days the scouts returned. They told that a large group of whitemen were coming in their direction. "These men are in great numbers," they said, "and they are building an iron road. To watch them from a distance is like watching flies swarm over something that has been left in the sun too long. The horses they use are not like ours. They have long ears, about the length from the elbow to the hand. Behind them on the iron road is a wagon with many wheels that makes a deafening noise. There is fire in the wagon, and big dark smoke comes from it. (From this description came the Saulteaux word *eshkoodayōdaban* – fire wagon – for the locomotive train.) Beyond all this is a big camp with many more whitemen." The scouts' report caused great concern. Some wanted to flee. Others, remembering the predictions of the forefathers, wanted to see this thing that had been foretold.

The elders of the band gathered together to decide what was to be done. Those that would flee were asked, "To where can you flee? Where are you going to hide?" Predictions had stated that in time the land would be covered with the whiteman in numbers far greater than the Indian. The elders decided that they should not bother the whiteman and hopefully they would leave the Indian alone. They also decided to watch this building of the iron road, warning particularly the young men to stay at a distance and not venture too close to the whiteman's camp.

As the days passed the cloud of smoke came closer. Finally one day they could see on the horizon the movements of many animals and men, and behind them, the smoke from the fire wagon. As the movements got closer each day, the air was filled with all kinds of sounds – whistles from the fire wagon, the shouts of men, and loud bangs of iron. From morning each day this sound continued till the night. There were many long-eared horses of different colours – black, brown, and even white ones. Some of the Indians amused themselves saying that the white ones must be giant jackrabbits found in the land where the whiteman came from. The coloured ones, they said, must have changed colour with the summer season. The camp that followed the iron road was large. Every four or five days this camp moved, as the building of the iron road moved further and further into the west. As the camp moved west curiosity got the better of two young men. Going against what they had been told, they decided to have a closer look at the camp. Leaving their camp unnoticed they approached the whiteman's camp. They noticed there were only a few men in camp. The rest had left to work on the iron road. As they stood close by the camp watching, a man came toward them from the camp. He held some sort of a bundle and gestured that he wanted them to have it. This man was different from the whiteman. He was a small man. He had no hair on his face and the black hair on his head was braided into one long braid that hung down his back. The man motioned for them to take the bundle and then placed it on the ground and headed back into camp. After much hesitation the two young men approached the bundle. Seeing it contained food, they took it. On their way to camp they sampled some of the food. It was tasty and they decided to share it with others in the camp. When they arrived in camp and told their story they received stern criticism for their actions. They were told the food must be thrown away for it might be poisonous. They were then given a large quantity of water and told to vomit, to empty their stomachs of the food they had eaten. The food that was thrown away provided much excitement for the camp dogs, who scrambled to get their share.

The strange man who had given them the food had been alluded to in predictions made in the past. With the coming of the whiteman, it had been foretold, many others would also come. Soon the land would be full of all kinds of people. To this strange man of the whiteman's camp the Indian gave the name "One Braid" because of the way he wore his hair. This was the first Chinese to meet the *Anishnaybay*.

THE LAST RAID

told by Earth Elder

Earth Elder, whose father Pinayzitt (Partridge Foot) was the hereditary chief of the band, recalled that Pinayzitt often led his people to Goose Lake. The lake, a natural habitat for waterfowl, was so named because every year it harboured many geese and waterfowl. Over the years, Pinayzitt's people came to know this area well. It was only natural, therefore, that when the treaties of 1870 were signed, the sons and nephews of Pinayzitt would take this area for their reserve.

With the formation of reserves a way of life was changed. The most fundamental change was from wandering to a life of confinement. Some things, however, did not change. Spirituality continued to be a major factor in everyday life. Rituals and dances of different kinds were still practised, one being the now long-forgotten mosquito dance. Personal commitments made prior to the reserve system were not forgotten; there was still the hope that one day they might be fulfilled. These commitments were usually

33

made in order to achieve a spiritual status which was necessary for direction and survival.

In the days when the whiteman had only been heard of, not yet seen, growing up to manhood meant only two things to the Anishnaybay – to be a hunter or a warrior. There was a third choice, which was to stay in camp with the women, but this was not considered honourable because it generally led to a later life of wifekeeping. Keshickasheway mingot (Blessed By the Sky), younger brother of Earth Elder, chose to be a warrior. Life for a warrior meant going on raiding ventures to penetrate an enemy camp and steal their horses. To do this enhanced the social position and wealth of the individual.

This story recounts an event which took place on the northeast shore of Goose Lake several winters after the Pinayzitt band had made their homes on their new reserve, which today is known as the Sakimay (Mosquito) Reserve. Earth Elder considered this an historic event because it was the last time such a commitment was carried out by any of his people.

At this time a message, accompanied by a tobacco offering, was sent to every home. It said, "*Acoose,* son of *Quewich,* has made a commitment to lead a group of men to challenge the unknown to the south, across the great Missouri River, to obtain horses." Earth Elder and his four brothers – Yellow Calf, Blessed By the Sky, *Akeyhasheway mingot* (Blessed by the Earth) and *Punnichienace* (New Born Bird) received the message. Only Blessed by the Sky accepted the challenge. Earth Elder and Yellow Calf were not in favour, saying that several winters had passed since a treaty had been made, in which it had been agreed that all fighting would stop, that they should live in peace on the land they had reserved for themselves. The treaty decreed that they were only to bear arms in defence of the land they had given up. Blessed by the Sky said that he agreed with *Acoose,* that commitments made to the Creator must be honoured. Other commitments were secondary. Both men committed to this venture expected their people to approve and support them in asking for guidance and protection from the Creator as it was customary to seek and receive this support.

Acoose announced that he and Blessed By the Sky would leave
when the spring break occurred and creeks began to flow.

During the winter, preparations were made. Many pairs of
mocassins were made, for their journey would take many days
of walking. Finally, the time came when the two were to leave.
On the eve before their departure a sing was held and prayers
were offered for their success. Unknown to the two a young
man in his teens had also made preparations to accompany
them in their venture. This young man was *Penipekeesik,* a
younger brother to *Acoose.* They warned him of the danger,
of the possibility of not returning. *Penipekeesik* insisted, and so
he was accepted as part of the group. Dawn came and they
left with *Acoose* leading, followed by Blessed by the Sky and
Penipekeesik in the rear. *Acoose* told his companions that there
was to be no looking back, for they must at all times pay attention to where they were going. At the same time they recognized that their lives were at the mercy of the Creator. They
travelled many days across the broad prairies, always keeping
a watchful eye for any movements, as there were already
whitemen in the area. Finally, in the distance they sighted a
row of hills. Beyond these hills was the great Missouri River
and across it the land where many horses were kept. After
entering the hill area they travelled many days, always watching for landmarks. Then one day they sighted the great
Missouri River. Now they looked for a camp with horses. For
this they had travelled many days. It was now early summer.
As they watched the river, they saw some distance downstream
a small wisp of smoke. This told them that there was a camp
at that point along the river. At dusk they reached a site across
the river from camp. There were many campfires in the camp.
From activity in the camp and from the absence of lookout
men they could tell that these Indians felt secure in their camp.
It was situated at a bend of the river; further downstream was
another bend. This is where the horses were kept. *Acoose* and
his companions observed the camp for several days, trying to
figure out the best way to approach the horses without rous-
ing too many men from the camp. During this time they fin-

ished the last of their food and had to resort to digging and eating wild turnips and berries, which were plentiful in the bushes around them. They dared not use the guns they carried to shoot the game they saw from time to time, or build a fire, for fear that the shots would be heard and the smoke would be seen. As hunger gnawed at their stomachs, they noticed that during the day the women from the camp would go to some scaffolds situated near some woods, climb the scaffolds and return to camp with bundles, after which campfires would be lit. When the wind came from the direction of the campfires they could smell the aroma of cooking meat and this made them very hungry.

Once, as they were watching the women returning from the scaffolds, *Penipekeesik* spoke, "Someone should go across the river and steal something to eat from the scaffolds, or do we stay here on this side and be hungry while there is something over there across the river?"

Acoose answered him, "My young brother, maybe you should go so we could eat."

Penipekeesik declined. Turning to Blessed by the Sky, *Acoose* then asked, "You, my cousin, would you go?"

Blessed by the Sky, knowing the authority of leadership said, "If you say I must go, then I will."

Acoose and Blessed By the Sky discussed ways and decided that the best time to go would be dusk, and the best way would be to walk beyond the spot he wanted to reach and then swim across the river. They knew that if he attempted to swim directly across from the camp, the current of the river would land Blessed By the Sky downstream from the camp, away from the scaffolds, which were located upstream from the camp. At dusk Blessed by the Sky walked upstream, selected a spot, and entered the river. As he swam, the current carried him to a spot not far from the scaffolds. Having reached the riverbank, he found a footpath used to carry water from the river to the camp. It was now dark and as he proceeded up the path he encountered no one. His curiosity led him to the outskirts of the camp. He saw people sitting around their campfires eating, talking, and laughing. Knowing that the scaffolds were unguarded he went in that direction. The scaffolds were higher than a man's height. He climbed up and once on top found bundles of dried meat. Taking two bundles he headed upstream and swam across the river. It was nearly dawn when he arrived, and they ate. He told his companions that the camp was unaware of their presence, but getting the horses across the river would be difficult due to the currents of the river.

More days passed as they watched the camp. One morning they saw a man come to the river and wade across. Directly below where they were hidden was a large flat area. This is where the man came. After putting up some saplings as markers the man returned to the river. By the man's actions they knew a camp site had been selected and in a few days the whole camp would move to this area. *Acoose* decided that it would be better to take the horses that would be brought over rather than risk driving the horses from the other side. Having decided on this, they waited. One day went by and early in the morning of the second day there was activity in the camp across the river. As they watched, a man riding a horse approached the river. He was followed by a woman, also on a horse, leading another horse with a travoise. As the couple made their way across the river, they knew this was no ordinary man, but a man of status, possibly a chief or a headman of the camp. They decided these were the horses they would take, for they knew men of status always owned good horses.

They watched as the woman erected a wigwam and the man tethered the horses. When the wigwam was fully erected the man and the woman both went inside. The time had come to make the attack. With gun in hand *Acoose* led the rush upon the wigwam. Reaching it he plunged inside. There was the sound of one shot. *Acoose* had killed the man. At that instant the woman escaped out the door, carrying a burning piece of wood which she hurled into the grass, starting a fire as a signal to those across the river. Alarmed by the sound of gun fire and the presence of the attacking men, two of the horses broke their tethers and fled beyond the reach of Blessed By the Sky and

Penipekeesik. In a desperate attempt to prevent all their spoils from eluding them, Blessed by the Sky shot the nearest horse. Running to it he cut off the tail. *Acoose,* already mounted on a sorrel horse, called to his companions to head north to a large hill they had seen about a half day's journey away. He would ride to the east as a decoy and then double back to the hill, where they would make a stand. The fire set by the woman was raging out of control between them and the river, but through the smoke they could see riders beginning to cross the river. As *Acoose* rode to the east, Blessed By the Sky and *Penipekeesik* took off, running as they had never run before. They dared not look back lest they lose time. They knew their lives depended on reaching that hill. After running a long time they saw the hill in the distance. Keeping an eye on the hill as they ran, they also watched for *Acoose.* There was no sign of him. Maybe he had been overtaken and met his end, they thought. All of a sudden, as if shot out of nowhere, they saw a rider on the hill before them. The two exhausted runners saw the rider wave and they knew it was *Acoose.* They tried to gain speed but it was impossible for they were very tired. Reaching the top of the hill, they saw in the east three clouds of dust, and knew they were from the riders who were chasing *Acoose.*

As they stood on the hill all seemed hopeless. They were in hill country, but there was no shelter. From the east their challenge was approaching. The unknown had now become real.

As they looked around, Blessed By the Sky spoke, "*Acoose,* we came to support you. If you fall we too shall fall. I cannot think that you brought us this far for nothing. You must know of a way to see us through."

There were tears in the eyes of the two as they waited for a response, for they knew *Acoose* was a man of physical and spiritual gifts.

Acoose answered, "If both of you will be seated and hold the horse, I will seek protection."

After they were seated *Acoose* took a small bundle that he carried on his back and opened it. It contained his pipe, sweetgrass and a stuffed chickadee.

He lit the sweetgrass and incensed his pipe, and said, "When I have filled and lit this pipe, I will speak to Him who made all the birds of the air, after which I will share this pipe with you. Do not move, no matter what you hear or see."

When he lit his pipe and began his prayer a mist came upon the hill. As the pipe was passed from person to person and smoked, the mist became thicker until it was almost like night. In the distance they could hear the sounds of horse hooves. As it came closer the sound became deafening. They could feel the ground shake as the riders bypassed the hill on both sides. Gradually the sounds diminished as the riders raced to the west. When the quiet had returned, the mist began to lift slowly. They got up and walked down the north side of the hill. At the base of the hill there were many hoof tracks, too many to count. The sun had now set. The three set their direction to the north. They knew they had to travel all night to put distance between them and this land where they would be hunted for what they had done. Riding the horse in turns they covered much ground during the night and when dawn came they looked for a place to hide and rest.

After hiding all day they continued after dark. Night travel was difficult so they decided they should take a chance and travel till midday and then rest. At last they reached the broad prairies. The hill country was now behind them. As the days went by the danger diminished and this allowed them to travel more slowly and search for food. They were able to kill small game and build fires to cook, until they ran out of powder for their guns. The guns were useless now to them but they carried them anyway. When they sighted game they would aim their guns in that direction and yell, "Bang!" The game of course continued on its merry way unharmed.

One day when *Penipekeesik* was riding the horse and acting as a lookout, he stopped the horse, pointed, and said, "Over there, there is a jackrabbit. *Acoose,* you say you are a fast runner. If this is true then we shall eat."

Acoose, recognizing this as a challenge to his ability to run, responded, "*Mechee* (brother) *Penipekeesik,* get off the horse if you must know how fast I can run. You will run with me. If you catch the rabbit then we shall eat."

Penipekeesik accepted the challenge. With Blessed By the Sky giving the signal, the race was on. The frightened jackrabbit took off, darting this way and that with the runners in hot pursuit. The race was evenly matched; neither of the two could gain on the other. Suddenly the rabbit made a sharp turn to *Penipekeesik's* side and he made a flying leap, catching the rabbit. After killing the rabbit *Penipekeesik* held it in the air above his head and yelled, "We eat! We eat!" The rabbit was given to Blessed By the Sky, who roasted it. When it was cooked *Penipekeesik* took his knife and cut it into three pieces.

He handed *Acoose* the hind quarter and to Blessed By the Sky he gave the front quarter. He took the middle, which is the back of the rabbit, and said, "I killed it so I should have the better part of the rabbit."

Each day as they travelled they recognized familiar landmarks, for this was the region where they had learned the ways of survival, where their fathers had hunted the buffalo which was no more. Early one day, they sighted a wisp of smoke coming from beyond a hill and going toward it, they could see a sod house. Not having eaten since the day before, they were hungry. They decided that one of them should go to the house and ask for food. It fell upon Blessed By the Sky to go. As he came near to the house, the door opened and a woman came out carrying an axe. She yelled something which he did not understand so he made a sign indicating that his stomach was empty. The woman hurried back into the house and came out carrying a bundle, which she placed a short distance from the house. She said something and made a sign for him to take it. He went to the bundle and saw that it was food. He then made some more signs that said there were two more and they were also hungry. He could see that the woman was afraid. She ran back into the house and came out carrying another bundle, which she placed some distance from him. She then walked back to the house and watched from the doorway as he took the bundle and walked back to where his companions waited, out of sight of the house. They went some distance before they stopped and opened the bundles. When they did, they found food, some tea and a twist of tobacco. After they had eaten and smoked, they continued. The tea they kept because they had no container in which to boil water.

The summer was coming to an end, as the three approached the lake from where they had departed in the spring. Entering their settlement and looking around they saw no one. Their houses were closed. Leaving the Goose Lake, they made their way north to where Earth Elder lived in a bush overlooking the Qu'Appelle Valley. They knew he would be at home and he was. Earth Elder told them that their wives, their children and nearly all the Indians from the reserve had left to visit the Leech Lakes, two days' journey to the north. After resting, visiting and telling Earth Elder of their adventures, they continued north to join their families. It is told that upon their arrival at the Leech Lake camp they were met with great joy. The horse tail that Blessed By the Sky had cut off the horse on the banks of the great Missouri River was hoisted on a pole and a great victory dance was held, lasting two days. So ends the story of the elders who lived on the shores of Goose Lake on the Sakimay Reserve, when the reserve was young. And so ended the last known expedition to challenge the unknown by any group of *Anishnaybak.*

THE GIFT OF THE
GRASS DANCE
told by Earth Elder

Grandfather Earth Elder, who was the eldest of five brothers, outlived all of them by many winters, reaching an age seldom reached by anyone in his band. During his last years Grandfather reminisced many times about his brothers, about where and how they had lived and things they had done that were important to him and his brothers. The brother next to Earth Elder had assumed the leadership of the band, after the passing of the their father, Pinayzitt. This brother, Osowopeeshkez (Yellow Calf), was an outspoken person, and because of this he experienced many difficult times in his role as leader. Keshickasheway mingot (Blessed By the Sky) who according to Indian tradition was considereed the elder of the twins because he was born first, also left his mark on the brothers, through his role as a warrior. He was remembered for accompanying a cousin on a raiding party to the south country to steal horses, after the reserve was settled. The younger of the twins, Akeyasheway mingot (Blessed

43

By the Earth), in the days before and after the reserve system was established, participated regularly in the dances and rituals of the people. But the important thing that Grandfather remembered about this brother was not what he did, but what he received. This is the story as told by Earth Elder about this brother.

When Grandfather began any story he always took great pains to explain why the story began as it did. In this particular story he told of people they met before the reserves were established, people with whom they shared food and experiences. Most of these people they met from time to time were Cree. Some of their men took wives from among the Cree. Later, when they went to the Qu'Appelle Valley to take part in the signing of the treaties, they made many new friends, some of whom were Assiniboine people. Grandfather explained that these people were settling in the area of a large wooded ridge, at a place a day's journey to the west of the new Saulteaux reserve at Goose Lake. Grandfather knew this land well as it lay due east from their favourite wintering camp and ancestral home at the Strawberry Lakes. It was a large wooded ridge about a day's journey in length from east to west with hills at the west end. He called it "Skulls of Men Ridge" because at certain locations on this ridge were found the remains of many Indians, who had been killed by the dreaded sickness smallpox.

As the seasons went by, Grandfather's people and the Assiniboine people often visited each other and they became well acquainted. Among these Assiniboine visitors was a young man named Walking Sun, who often came with his father. Walking Sun became very friendly with Grandfather Earth Man and his brothers. Unknown to the brothers, Walking Sun recognized a brother among them. His own brother had passed on before the Assiniboine people moved to their new reserve. When Walking Sun told his father that among Earth Man and his brothers, he had recognized his own brother, the elder was overjoyed. He told his son that in the near future they would go and make official adoption. (At this point in the story, Grandfather explained that Indians of various tribes practised this custom. When they recognized a person who had the same features as the person they had lost, they adopted this person.

In the adoption ceremony, a gift of great significance was given to the person who was adopted. The adoption was binding for a lifetime and was recognized by members of both families.) As this custom directed, Walking Sun and his father journeyed to Goose Lake to visit Earth Man and his brothers. At the appropriate time, Walking Sun's father approached the brothers and announced, "Among your numbers, my son has recognized a brother." The brother that was recognized was the younger twin, Blessed By the Earth, later known as *Sanquis* – a Saulteaux word for mink. Walking Sun's father was not only an Assiniboine elder, he was a headman of the Grass Dance Society among his own people, so the gift he gave his new-found son was the ceremony called the grass dance. Before this time Grandfather and his people had other dances but not the grass dance. In the Assiniboine elder's instruction on the use of his gift, he told Blessed By the Earth of its religious significance, and how and when it was to be held. He told his new son to carry this dance and ceremony during the remainder of his life and eventually in the future to pass it on to his children and his people.

When Grandfather Earth Man spoke about this brother and how he used the gift given to him, he summed it up like this, "My younger brother loved his dance because it was a great gift, which he shared with all the people. From it, the people got hope and life not only for themselves, but for their children."

THE LAST GRASS DANCE
told by Standing Through the Earth

Grandfather Standing Through the Earth was an elder who was knowledgeable about many things, both social and spiritual, and their application to the traditional and cultural ways of our people. Many times during his life I found him to be strange. Maybe this was because he was of one era and I was of another.

Whenever I would ask Grandfather a question that was of a humourous nature, his response was immediate. Sometimes he would ask Grandmother to provide an answer. Whenever I asked questions that dealt with the facts of life, Grandfather was quick to respond, "A'how, Medimoya (all right, old lady), our grandson wants to know, tell him what he wants to know." Usually this amused him and he laughed.

Then there were times I would ask a certain kind of question and receive no immediate response. Instead he would remain motionless, and after a period of silence, he would say, "There is a period in the life of every

47

person in which there is foolishness. When this period passes some peo-
ple will grow up, remembering and using what they were told. For this
we have a saying, 'When you have had enough foolishness, then you
become knowledgeable and know your mistakes.' There are others who
never go beyond this first stage; they remain foolish for the rest of their
lives. To those people we say, 'Your foolishness will accompany you to
your old age.'"

When I received this kind of response I was forced to practice patience
and wait for a later time to ask my question. Very early in life I learned
not to ask questions about spiritual things—particularly those things directly
related to Grandfather or any other older person. These things, I was
told, were very personal and were to be held in utmost respect. They were
only alluded to in story form. Ceremonies and rituals were never described
in detail. To ask old people questions about their spiritual attributes was
unthinkable.

When I first asked Grandfather about the grass dance I already knew
some things about it. From the stories told by Grandfather Earth Elder
I knew where it had come from, and how it had come. On occasions
when I asked my mother about it she only told me who performed the
dance, not how or why the dance was performed. To these questions,
she always replied, "Ask your grandfather, he was part of it."

Once she made a comment that revealed her recollection of that period,
"The dancer who wore the eagle belts in the grass dance looked beautiful.
They were good dancers, very quick and beautiful to watch."

My desire to know about the grass dance was to be satisfied one day.

It was a day in early summer. In the morning I helped Grandfather hitch his ponies to the wagon. After this was done I
was told to help load the wagon with the berry-picking pails,
some water containers, and a box of food. I was told that my
mother and grandmother were going to pick saskatoon berries
and Grandfather was going to chop willow pickets for fence
posts. I was to help him. I was to be the pack horse who pulled the pickets out of the bush as they were cut, a job I wasn't
really looking forward to. After hours of going from this bush
to that bush, and finding only a few pickets, we came upon
the Goose Lake from a northerly direction. We were on an

abandoned trail along what was once the northwestern shoreline of Goose Lake. Suddenly Grandfather pulled his ponies to a stop and said, *"Medimoyea* (old lady), remember a long time ago when the shoreline was here and there were many kinds of summer fowl on the lake? At times there were so many geese they looked like snow upon the water."

After the old people reminisced for several minutes about the old days we continued along what used to be the lake shore. A short time later we came upon a small clearing between two fairly large patches of trees and bushes. This was the place where the old log hall had stood by the shores of Goose Lake. The old hall was now gone.

As we approached the site I began to remember something about this place. The winter before I went to boarding school we came here once to watch a dance which I knew was the grass dance. We lived about three quarters of a mile north of here, and the whole family piled into the sleigh to make this trip. That evening and night were very cold. I knew it was very cold because from the time we left our house till we got here I was completely covered in blankets. I could not see anything. All I could hear was the sound of sleigh runners as they slid along the snow, and the sound of harness tugs as the horse pulled the sleigh.

When we arrived and went into the hall, we saw many people with children and many old people. Grandfather was there, so was Grandmother. My mother told me to sit in one place and to be quiet during the entire time we would be there. I cannot remember any of the other children making noise or running about either.

As we waited quietly for what was about to take place, I saw Grandfather dressed in a white traditional costume sitting by the door. To his left, and coming from the far opposite side of the hall, was the sound of bells and the aroma of burning sweet grass. A drum was placed in the centre of the hall. All was quiet. Then one of our grandfathers, whom I knew quite well, said a prayer. His name, the name I always called him, was *Wahpossway* (Old Man Bunnie).

I remembered seeing men seated on the floor around the drum. These were the singers. To one side of the singers stood another of the grandfathers, a brother to Grandfather Standing Through the Earth. His name was North Wind. This grandfather never danced. All he did was stand by the drum throughout the entire dance. The singing began and the dancers began their dance. During parts of the dance they danced slowly and at other times very fast. They let out shouts as they danced round and round the drum. On the ladies' side of the hall some elderly women stood dancing in one place. All at once there was a great shout. The dancers stopped dancing and the singers stopped singing.

There was something going on behind the drum and dancers that I could not see. Then the singing began again. This time some other men danced, just plain men. They carried ladles which they waved as they shouted.

The best part came after the dance was finished. Food was served, along with apples and bags of candy. My mother told me not to eat right away, first we had to listen. I remembered listening to another grandfather speak for a long time. He talked about us children and other children. This grandfather talked for such a long time, I couldn't hold out, I just had to dig into the candy. I'm sure I was not the only child to do this. I didn't remember what happened after that. I do know that a social dance followed—a round dance. I awoke the next morning back at our house. I knew that it had not been a dream because I still had some candy and apples.

As we neared the site where the old log hall had stood, Grandfather pulled his ponies to a turn and made for the edge of the bush.

There in the shade of the trees and bushes Grandfather stopped and said, "We will stop here and eat." Pointing to the bush along the lake bed, he said, "The saskatoons used to be good here."

We all got off the wagon and I helped Grandfather unhitch his ponies. In a short time a fire was built, the tea made, and we all sat down to eat. As we ate I thought again about the old log hall, about the time we came here during that one winter. In my mind I debated whether I should ask or not.

Finally I turned to my mother, "Should I ask Grandfather about the old hall and what happened when we came here that one winter?"

Without saying a word she took out her tobacco, placed a pipeful in my hand, and said, "Here. Ask him."

As I was about to offer the tobacco to Grandfather my mother spoke to him. "He wants to ask you about the old hall and about the last time there was a grass dance here."

With a look on his face that suggested he was deep in thought, Grandfather took the tobacco.

"*Noozis* (grandchild)," he said, "you have given me much tobacco in the past. I have told you stories. These stories I have told you were stories by the old men (elders) who lived here at Goose Lake since the reserve was here. Some of these stories were told when there was no reserve, no whiteman, so long ago we don't know when.

"This," he said, pointing to the sky and around him, "what you see around you is a story. What the *Anishnaybay* does and how he lives is a story. You, in time to come, will tell about me. Your children will tell about you—if you are foolish or not foolish—whatever they say about you will be a story. When your grandchildren come you will look back. You will see and know many things. This will be your story. What you ask I will tell you.

"Long ago when your grandmother and I were young, we came here to Goose Lake. (Grandfather was originally from the Riding Mountain area in central Manitoba and Grandmother came from the Turtle Mountains in Dakota Territory.) The people here at Goose Lake already had the grass dance. The elder *Sanquis,* father of my son-in-law, *Macheeaniquot* (Floating Cloud), had the ceremony. Elder *Sanquis* lived west of here at the other lake and had a big house. Round dances were held there and sometimes at mid-winter the grass dance was held there. I am told he got the dance as a gift from the Assiniboine people. This hall that was here was not the first.

There was another across the lake to the east side. It was not really a hall but a big house.

"To have a part in the ceremony of the grass dance is an honour. In this dance there were four dancers, four singers, and four servers. There were speakers, a keeper of the drum, which at that time was *Mechee* (brother) *Keewaytinopeenace* (North Wind), and a keeper of the door. I was the last keeper of the door. When everyone who was to take part in the dance was ready, my part was to shut the door. I didn't let anyone in or out until the dance was over. When the door was shut a pipe was given to a speaker. Before the Elder *Sanquis* passed on, this was his part, as leader and headman of the Grass Dance Society. There had been other speakers in the past, like the father of *Nokeequon* (Soft Feather), Jim Bunnie. The speaker prayed to the Thunder Bird Eagle to bless the men who were holding the eagle belts which they were going to wear. These belts were sacred and used only for this dance. I have never been given the right to wear the eagle belt, only the eagle feather hat that I still have today. He also prayed for the keeper of the drum and the men seated around the drum. Four rainbows were painted on the drum, one for each direction, and at each direction sat a singer. The keeper of the drum stood at the east side of the drum. On the women's side stood four elderly women. They were noted in the community for their generosity and sharing with others. For these women, too, the speaker prayed. And for the children, and for all children yet to come. He prayed that each would be blessed with a head of grey and a long life.

"When this was done the dancers put on their belts. The dance was ready to begin. These belts came from an eagle that had been skinned, removing the head, the legs, the wings, and some of the tail feathers, and leaving only the back. From this section the belt was made and then decorated with ribbons of different colours.

"There were four main songs in this dance. The keeper of the drum kept track of them by passing a certain number of sticks from one hand to the other. The last two songs were sung twice. When the keeper of the drum held up four sticks in each hand we knew that this was the last part of the ceremony. This song was very fast and the dancers had to be very quick. The song ended when the lead dancer, who carried a sharpened stick, pierced a portion of the contents of a kettle, and held it up for all to see. The kettle held a cooked young dog that had been raised and prepared for this purpose. The lead dancer then took an eagle feather and dipped the tip of it into the broth and dropped one drop onto the tongue of each of his fellow dancers. Another song was sung to which the four men danced. They were the servers; their work, then, was to serve the food to the people.

"When this song was ended all the members of the Grass Dance Society were served the contents of the kettle. When the meal was ended the chief of the band, or some other headman, recounted why this ceremony was held – it meant that one half of the winter was now past. The hardships of the second half would soon be over. With the coming of the spring it would be as morning after a dark night. We would be glad when the grandfathers[1], among whom would be Thunder Bird Eagle, would come to give rain and life to all things, and we, too, the *Anishnaybak* would have life."

When Grandfather had finished his story, he added the comment, "Because of the changing times and forces outside our community, the Indians of tomorrow will never see, only hear of, the sacred ceremony and ritual called the grass dance."

---

1. Grandfathers, as used here, denotes Thunderbirds, the rolling thunder of the early spring, among whom, it was said, was the Eagle Thunder Bird.

YELLOW CALF

told by Earth Elder

Earth Man often mentioned his brother Osowopeeshkez (Yellow Calf) in his stories. When he spoke of Yellow Calf he was speaking of a time when crucial decisions had to be made for the well-being and future survival of his band. At that time they were known as the Pinayzitt People, because their father, Pinayzitt, was the original hereditary chief of their band. The following is Earth Man's account of Yellow Calf's role in the Treaty negotiations and the events which followed.

After *Pinayzitt's* tracks came to an end, the question of leadership arose. This was after Earth Man's bout with the dreaded smallpox, and after his self-imposed isolation of three summer and two winter seasons. He was past forty winters at this time. Although tribal custom directed that, as the eldest male of the family, he should succeed his father as chief, Earth Man

55

declined the position. He stated that he had no desire to be a chief. His role as hunter and provider for his people was the most important thing in his life. The problem of appointing a new hereditary chief continued unsettled right up to the time of departure for the Qu'Appelle Valley, where the treaties were to be signed.

In the absence of a chief, the family delegated Yellow Calf to sit as their representative in the negotiations. Earth Man said, in his Saulteaux tongue, *"Ikeywetubpeeman Ogemacanan Nayacwong wochee,"* which told us that Yellow Calf sat with Chief *Waywayscappo*, the grandfather of the present-day *Anishnaybak* of the *Waywayscappo* band in western Manitoba. The word, *Nayacwong* (Point of Wooded Bluff) is the Saulteaux name for the land now known as the *Waywayscappo* Reserve. At the actual signing of the treaties Yellow Calf did not record his signature. This was done by others including Chief *Waywayscappo*.

From the time of their arrival in the Qu'Appelle Valley until many of the agreements were complete, an entire spring and summer had passed. Of the many issues discussed, two were outstanding in Grandfather Earth Man's mind. One was what he called "the one big money" issue. This was a sum of five dollars to be paid annually to each status Indian. Earth Man made it clear that, had they known the value of money and what it would do in future times, they would not have agreed to a fixed amount. No amount of money could ever compensate for the value of the land, even at ploughshare depth, or the way of life that was lost.

The other issue was the question of what land the band would receive. Earth Man described the land they were to be given as an *"Eshquoneegun"* (that which is left), a reserve. The band was informed that naming a chief or headman was the first requirement for being assigned a reserve. Faced with this situation, the *Pinayzitt* people were forced to name a chief. Both Earth Man and Yellow Calf declined the position because they felt they were too young. They respected the custom that an elder, one with wisdom and experience, should fill the posi-

tion. Finally, the decision was made that the responsibility of
headman would go to an older man whose name was *Sikemay*
(the original Saulteaux word for mosquito, today written as
Sakimay). *Sikemay* was a cousin to the family and a nephew
to Earth Man's late mother. The land the band chose was the
area surrounding Goose Lake. It was land well known to them,
since before the coming of the whiteman. With the choice of
this land their name as a band was changed from the *Pinayzitt*
people to the Goose Lake people.

In telling the story of the last raid, Earth Man was also describ-
ing the changes that were taking place at this time. Stressing
the importance of commitment in traditional Indian culture,
he told the story of the two men—one, his brother
Keshickasheway mingot (Blessed By the Sky), and the other, his
cousin *Acoose*. As a young man many winters before the formation of reserves, *Acoose* had sworn a personal commitment
to lead a group of men on a horse-stealing raid. The Indian
of that day had the ability to predict events that were going
to occur, but could not predict how the event would affect
them. To take part in a horse-stealing raid, therefore, was to
challenge the unknown, and to admit that he depended heavily
on his spiritual gifts, his physical ability and the mercy of his
Creator. Once such a commitment was made, it was considered
binding between him and his Creator. When *Acoose* announced
his intentions, Earth Man and his brothers were divided in their
response to this venture.

Blessed By the Sky supported *Acoose* and was ready to go
with him, for he was a warrior. He had already in the past
gone to the land beyond the Great *Peiganoweceepeeg* (Missouri
River) to steal horses from other hostile Indian tribes.

Earth Man consulted with Yellow Calf, and after discussing
the matter they approached the two men, *Acoose* and Blessed
By the Sky, who were committed to the raiding venture.
Yellow Calf reminded them that several winters had passed
since the signing of the treaties. He and the other chiefs and
headmen who had negotiated the treaties, had been given to
understand that the Great Lady Chief (Queen) in the land

beyond the great waters would look after their needs, and that they, the *Anishnaybak,* must stop all hostility and live in peace with each other. It had been agreed that in the future none of their Indian children would ever be compelled to bear arms and to fight. *Acoose* and Blessed By the Sky insisted that a personal commitment to the Creator was more important. It remained to be seen whether the promises made to them in the treaties would be kept. Yellow Calf's response was, "What was honourable in times past is now and in the future wrong because of our commitment to a treaty, as a people." After much discussion by the family, *Acoose* and Blessed By the Sky were allowed to go, for the sake of family relationship and unity.

Earth Man said Yellow Calf had remarkable speaking abilities, as well as other great leadership qualities. When Yellow Calf made a statement it was direct, straight from the shoulder and final. His attitude was considered radical because he spoke candidly about what he saw, and critically about his people's confinement within a reserve. This was used against him later by whitemen of authority. They knew they were dealing with an Indian with ideas, but they treated him as an incompetent savage.

Earth Man described an incident in which Yellow Calf sought to obtain tools from the Indian agent with which to begin tilling the soil on the reserve. The Indian agent was prepared to give little more than a handful of grain, saying, "Here, go ahead and cultivate for your survival."

By this time, the formerly abundant game was scarce and hunting was limited to within the reserve. Yellow Calf and his people knew they would starve waiting for sufficient amounts of grain to feed them. The question was asked among the people, "How many winters must we wait for enough grain to grow and be sufficient to feed us?"

In this, as in other related matters, Yellow Calf felt that the local government officials were failing to comply with the provisions of the treaties. This angered Yellow Calf to the point of frustration and disgust. Earth Man made no mention of any actual skirmishes involving Yellow Calf and the government officials of the day. He did say, however, that prior to his departure, Yellow Calf did taunt certain government officials whom he disliked and for whom he had no respect, because of their inability to live up to their responsibilities under the treaties. The coalition of local government officials and the clergy caused him great concern. He saw the spiritual unity of his people disintegrating, leaving them in a state of confusion and uncertainty. In view of these deteriorating conditions, Yellow Calf decided to depart from his people, rather than suffer further degradation under government and church pressures.

After leaving his people Yellow Calf lived for many years with the Chippewa people of the Turtle Mountains in North Dakota. He is remembered in that country as a very old man, an excellent storyteller, who was respected by many. Near the end of his days Yellow Calf returned to Canada to the reserve named after his old ally and relative, Chief *Waywayscappo*. On the *Waywayscappo* Reserve at Rossburn, Manitoba, the path of the old man called *Osowopeeshkez* (Yellow Calf) came to an end. He was buried in a Presbyterian cemetery there.

Hilda *(Osowwaycekak)* Pelltier, an elder in her nineties and the last surviving member of the *Akeywakeyazee* (Earth Man – Earth Elder) family of the Cowessess Band in Saskatchewan, responded this way when asked about Yellow Calf. "Our father[1] *Osowopeeshkez* was a smart man. There have not been many Indian leaders like him."

---

1. In times past the *Anishnaybak* used the terms father and mother in referring to their uncles and aunts. This was still her way. Yellow Calf was Hilda's uncle but she still called him father.

THE LAST RAIN DANCE
told by Standing Through the Earth

Standing Through the Earth told another story from the time when Yellow Calf was having so much trouble with government and church authorities. This event had repercussions for the spiritual life of the Anishnaybay from which he has never fully recovered. In recalling this period, Standing Through the Earth explained that schools had already been established in the area. The McKay Mission (Presbyterian) was at the east end of Round Lake and twenty miles away there was a Roman Catholic Mission at the east end of Crooked Lake, both in the Qu'Appelle Valley. Local government officials and the Roman Catholic clergy were putting pressure on the Goose Lake people to abandon their tribal customs and beliefs. The missionary McKay, who worked mainly with Cree Indians in his area, made occasional visits to Goose Lake and the surrounding country, but he put little pressure upon the Indians he visited.

The Goose Lake People still held to the beliefs and practices that had

61

been handed down to them by their forefathers for countless generations. Many of the men and women were still spiritually gifted and understood the wonders of nature and the mysteries of life and death and could predict future events. They practised strict discipline in their observances of ceremonies, rituals and dances. This kept them spiritually stable and in unity with each other. In spite of the pressure that was applied by the missionaries and the government, the Goose Lake people continued to practise and to perform dances of various kinds. They held the buffalo dance, the horse dance, the bear dance, the warrior dance (also known as the one-legged dance), the round dance and the now-forgotten mosquito dance. These ritualistic dances had great spiritual significance.

Among the Goose Lake People there were also men and women who belonged to the Medewin (Grand Medicine Lodge). These members were knowledgeable in herbal remedies, and in the mysteries and wonders of nature and creation. Their main religious ceremony was the rain dance. Spiritual elders who could perform this ceremony at this period were few and far between, so the rain dance was not held often. Because the calendar system as we know it today was not used then, the announcement of the event might tie it to when certain berries were ripe or when the leaves on the trees reached the size of a man's ear. In the rain dance the rituals of rope-pulling and the buffalo head-pull were practised in a rigourous and disciplined manner.

In this story Standing Through the Earth told of the rain dance which was to be the last one held anywhere for many years.

The first part of the rain dance was the buffalo head-pull. The men who had committed themselves would have the skin on their backs pierced at the shoulder blades. Buffalo skulls, numbering anywhere from two to four or even more, would be fastened to the pierced skin on their shoulder blades with rawhide ropes. They would then pull these buffalo skulls into the encampment where the rain dance was being held. The ritual demanded that the participants be clean in body, mind and spirit. This ritual, attributed to Grandfather Buffalo and his children, was not to be taken lightly. Only those who had experienced a vision of mercy from Grandfather Buffalo were entitled to participate in the buffalo head-pull. As a young man at this time, Standing Through the Earth was committed to this ritual. He fulfilled his commitment at this rain dance, pulling six buffalo skulls.

On the morning following the day when the buffalo head-pull was held there was to be the rope-pulling ritual. The participants would be ready at daybreak, the ritual would begin at sunrise. For this ceremony the participants would have their shoulders pierced on the front side, where rawhide ropes would be fastened. The other ends of the ropes were tied to the sacred grandfather tree, which stood in the centre of the rain dance lodge. The dance involved pulling back and sideways. Standing Through the Earth stressed that this ceremony was painful and required great meditation and commitment. This dance, he said, was the greatest sacrifice of pain and suffering the *Anishnaybay* could offer his Creator. He did it for blessing and prosperity for himself and his children.

There were rumours that high-ranking government officials would be present at this particular ritual. Hearing this, the elder who was performing the rain dance ceremony advised those who had prepared not to perform the rope-pulling ceremony. He cautioned that up to this time the pressure imposed upon them to give up their way of life and worship was not enforced by the law, but if anything should go wrong it would give the government and Church an excuse to enact laws prohibiting the practice of their tribal customs and beliefs.

The rumours were true. On that day two buggies arrived bearing members of the North-West Mounted Police and goverment officials. They were escorted into the rain dance lodge and given places to sit. It was explained to them that fasting and dancing for a period of two nights and two days were the main elements of the rain dance. The purpose of the dance, they were told, was to ask for rain so that the earth might be replenished. They were also told that the rain dance was not held every year, because there were few spiritual elders who could perform the ceremony.

While the officials were watching the ceremony, a man entered the rain dance lodge. He had with him tobacco and a pair of rawhide ropes. There was nothing that could be done to stop him. He was already in the area of the sacred grandfather tree. He was not a member of the Goose Lake people, but was known to them. His name was *Osowwahshtim* (Brown Horse). The man announced that he had come to fulfill a commitment, that the whiteman present should know the spiritual strength of the Indian. With great reluctance his shoulders were pierced and fastened to the rawhide ropes. The other ends were tied to the sacred grandfather tree. The singing began. Brown Horse jumped back and began his dance. His jumps were rapid, backwards and sideways. All of a sudden the skin on his shoulders gave way and broke. He fell with a thud and lay unconscious and bleeding at the feet of one of the officials. The startled official jumped up, enraged by what he had just witnessed. The rain dance was stopped right there. Several arrests were made. Those arrested were put in bonds and made to walk behind the buggies, and were led away to jail. A ban was put on all Indian ceremonies which was to last many, many years.

"This happened right here," Standing Through the Earth said, "at the fork of the last creek in the southeast corner of our reserve."

He concluded by saying that in the years since this occurred the *Anishnaybay* have lost much. Because the traditional ceremonies and rituals were no longer practised, he said, many of our people do not know their language or the value life gives to everyone.

THE LAST DAYS OF
THE HUNTER

told by Alexander Wolfe

When Grandfather Earth Man told of his people and their coming to the place where the Sakimay Reserve is today in south-central Saskatchewan, he called this place, "Nekeesacaguneeg" a name given to the land in which the lake called "Nekeesacagun" (Goose Lake) is found. Grandfather recalled how his father Pinayzitt had led his people to this lake many times before the coming of the whiteman. During Earth Man's lifetime on the reserve and in the years after he passed on in 1937 these Saulteaux names continued to be used. They were dropped from usage about thirty years ago. Since then the Goose Lake people have become known simply as the Sakimays from the Sakimay Reserve.

Grandfather Earth Man had hunted and periodically lived near Goose Lake, where food and game were plentiful. His permanent home, however, was at the north end of what was to become the Sakimay Reserve, overlooking the Qu'Appelle Valley. It was here that Grandfather Earth Man was *to spend the last days of the many winters his Creator had bestowed upon him, and here that I saw him for the last time.*

When the lady Grandfather was destined to grow old with, Grandmother *Ogemabetung,* passed on, Grandfather built the last of his many dwellings. It was a small house, very simple. A door to the south and two small windows – one to the east and the other to the west. The furnishings, too, were simple – a small metal bed, which he never used, preferring to sleep on the floor by the stove, a small wooden table and a bench. These were also seldom used by Grandfather, for he preferred to eat sitting on the floor as he had done all his life. On the wall directly above where Grandfather had his bed hung two guns. The older one, the one with a broken stock, has its story, the other was of a newer type. The only thing in the house that he used continuously was a cast iron stove. This stove was about two feet long and a foot wide. It looked like a box held up by legs about eight inches off the floor. At one end was a door through which Grandfather put wood into the fire. The stove was used for heat and for cooking. In the evenings and sometimes at night Grandfather left the door of the stove open, so that the fire inside the stove gave light to the spot where Grandfather slept. It was from this spot that Grandfather Earth Man told his many stories. Some of his stories had been handed down to him by his father and grandfathers, others were his own stories about his life.

Fifty winters have passed since Grandfather Earth Man came to the end of the path on which his grandfathers walked. Nearing the end of this path he spoke many times of those *pickinowinnoun,* the Saulteaux word for seasons, and of his hope that his grandchildren would experience many more. Grandfather himself had experienced many seasons as they passed during his lifetime, which lasted more than a hundred winters. It was difficult for me to imagine that Grandfather had lived so long and had been a hunter, a person who could run and walk great distances. When I stood beside him, he was only two hands taller than I (and I was only a boy at the time) because his frame was stooped with age. Through his role as hunter, provider of food for his people, Grandfather Earth Man came to know landmarks, rivers and lakes where food and game were to be found, and distant sites which were considered sacred by his people. He knew the spot where the Rock with Written Symbols was found, known today as the Writing Rock Historical Site, nestled among the rolling hills of northwestern North Dakota. When they were hungry and desperate, spiritual instinct sometimes led grandfather and other Indians to the place called *Peeshkeekatat* (Lodge of the Buffalo), where Grandfather Buffalo dwelt. This hill stands alone on the Dakota plains in central North Dakota. To the west, Grandfather said, is a great ridge reached only after many days of travel across the plains and along many ridges of hills. When one views this great ridge in the distance from the east, past midday it looks like a dark low cloud on the western horizon. This darkness, he said, is created by the trees of many different kinds which grow there. Grandfather and his people often went to hunt there because there was much game in this place, known today as the Cypress Hills in southwestern Saskatchewan.

When Grandfather settled down comfortably on his spot in front of the stove he often raised the topic of manhood. A man, Grandfather said, does useful things for others and is responsible in all his dealings with his fellow beings and all creation. When he was young, Grandfather said, the grandfathers and grandmothers told him many things, and their advice had proved very useful. It gave him wisdom and sound judgement for the many decisions he was to make later in life. One piece of advice he had received and to which he attributed his long life was this: the mind and body work together and they must be allowed to develop fully if there is to be a long and useful life.

Grandfather was very critical of and disturbed by what he saw around him in his later years. He said, "Children today are not taking the time to become fully developed before they start having their own children. Blood relationship is ignored, relatives are having children." Grandfather said this was bad for the offspring. In times past, when relationship was held in honour and respect, and intermarriage did not occur, the blood of the *Anishnaybay* was pure and strong. This made him hardy in mind and body. When Grandfather spoke of child-bearing and the responsibility of raising the young, he often referred to the story of Grandfather Buffalo and the Orphan Children. In that story, the boy and girl were being cared for by their aunt very poorly and as a result the children had to wander around trying to feed themselves. Grandfather Buffalo takes the children, teaches them and then sends them back. This story, he said, came from the time when the *Anishnaybay* began to ignore what he had been in early times. This was why Grandfather Buffalo cared for and instructed the two children and then sent them back to teach their people.

In his many accounts of manhood before the coming of the whiteman, Grandfather Earth Man used to say, "There were different kinds of men, but three types were generally recognized. There was the kind that never went anywhere. This kind of man spent most of his time in the wigwam, day after day. He was called a wife-keeper. This man had no shame. He was very possessive of his wife, jealous not only of men but even of her contacts with other women. He was known to accompany his wife even in her personal matters, like going out to relieve herself. This sort of man," Grandfather said, "had to be given food from the hunt lest he got hungry and starved in camp. This was because he did nothing but keep his wife day after day."

Then there were the warriors. "These men," Grandfather said, "were held in high esteem within the band. These men were brave and usually very gifted spiritually. They went on raiding parties and brought back the spoils, usually in horses. These were the men who led the victory dances and told of their heroic deeds and narrow escapes in enemy territory. They were also the scouts who ventured out to meet the challenges, when the camp was threatened by unknown forces. When in camp they spent much of their time on high ground, scanning the horizon. In those days," Grandfather said, "one never knew when or from where some unfriendly stranger would appear. This was why these men were always on the lookout."

Then there was the hunter. This was Grandfather's role throughout his life, from the time he learned how to use the bow at an early age. "Hunting," he said, "involved much walking and sometimes running great distances, in any season." Bringing back what he had killed was often very difficult because of distance and weather. When large animals like moose, elk or buffalo were his kill, he would take as much as he could carry back to camp. Arriving at camp, he would tell the people of his kill and its whereabouts and they would then go and get what he had killed. This Grandfather Earth Man called "*neequoneeso,*" a Saulteaux word meaning to retrieve or to go and get what was left behind.

In the winter season, skinning a large animal was difficult because of the cold. To keep his hands warm while skinning, Grandfather said he would shove them under the hide of the animal, usually around the stomach, allowing the animal's body heat to warm them. He did this periodically until he was finished skinning the animal, then he would cut the meat so it could be carried. Grandfather never mentioned using a horse to carry his kill, it was always by backpack. As the seasons changed, Grandfather went to different places in his search for game. The spring and summer seasons took him to the lakes and rivers and occasionally to the wide open space of the Great Plains. The fall and winter season led him to the woodlands on the ridges of the land on which he and his people roamed. Grandfather's great knowledge, gained from experience, directed him to the kind of animal or bird that was good to eat in each season.

In the last years of his life Grandfather depended largely on the rations provided twice a month by the local farm instructor. This ration consisted of about ten pounds of flour and about a pound each of tea, dry beans, rice and rolled oats. In the spring and summer he received a small slab of salt pork, about five pounds. The pork was so heavily coated with salt it had to be boiled twice and the water dumped out before it could be cooked and eaten. In the fall and winter Grandfather was also given a hunk of beef, about five to ten pounds, depending on the supply on hand at the ration house. I was told that this beef was bought by the government from the local Indians, to be given to the old people and widows. In fact, the meat was not always used for this purpose. The Indians on the reserve at that time had many cattle, numbering I was told several hundred head. But these cattle could not be freely sold. Government policy called for strict regulation of sales by Indians. They were not allowed to sell produce like grain and livestock, or natural resources like hay, wood or fence posts, without a permit. The issue of a permit was at the discretion of the local farm instructor. If he didn't like you, the permit was refused; if he liked you the permit was granted on a limited basis.

By this time Grandfather's way of life and his diet had changed drastically. His hearing and eyesight had greatly diminished and the movements of his limbs were weakened by his advanced age. He could no longer provide for himself as he had done in times past. The meat that was issued to him during the fall and winter was not the meat to which he was accustomed. Even the name he gave to the cattle from which the beef came, was different from that of the majestic buffalo. The Saulteaux word used to describe the buffalo was *muskoday pesheekey*. The cattle he called *awacanee pesheekey*. *Awacan* is a Saulteaux word used to describe a person or animal that has been denied its freedom and confined to a limited environment. The word *muskoday* describes an open plain such as the prairie where the buffalo in times past roamed in freedom.

But Grandfather's way of sharing in times past had not been in vain. Now people would stop by and give him the wild meat that he loved. When this happened, Grandfather was always grateful and told his visitors a story.

Grandfather Earth Man was a storyteller who could tell the stories of long ago, but, like most Indians, he also loved to tell a humourous story on occasion. One such story that he told was about how he embarrassed the local farm instructor and his wife one hot summer afternoon. Directly behind Grandfather's house to the north was a road that went down through a ravine to the Crooked Lake. At the lake were numerous cottages and a store. During the mid-summer, particularly on Sunday afternoon, the place was alive with activity. White people from the communities surrounding the reserve and from neighbouring towns would come to enjoy an afternoon of swimming and fishing. On this particular day, Grandfather – who was unaware that it was Sunday – was going about his daily routine. Near the head of his bed were two duffle bags, one of which contained his personal belongings, and the other he used to keep treats for his grandchildren when they came to visit. This bag was also the place where he kept the ginger ale that he liked. On this day, while checking this bag, he noticed that he was out of his favourite drink. He decided to walk down to the store in the valley. He then discovered that he had only one piece of clean clothing and it was not something he had ever worn. This piece of clothing had been part of the supplies issued to him the previous fall, when supplies had been given to the band. At that time the government held money in trust for Indians on reserves and doled out this money in the form of supplies, as it saw fit. The supplies were usually given out in the fall and consisted of mackinaw coats, wool socks, wool pants and fleece-lined combination underwear for the men. The women received yard goods, usually flannel, knitting yarn with knitting needles and grey wool blankets with the letters I.D. (Indian Department) stamped on them. Shotgun shells, twenty-two bullets and snare wire were also given to each family. Grandfather knew what to do with the coats, socks, pants and blankets. But he was puzzled by the combination underwear, as he had never seen such a thing in his life. It was one of those kind that had three buttons in the back on the waistline, holding up a flap which was to be unbuttoned and let down when nature called. When Grandfather asked about its use, the farm instructor had told him it was to be worn. Now Grandfather was faced with a decision. Should he venture out in soiled clothing or should he wear the only piece of clean clothing he had, namely the fleece-lined combination underwear? After some thought he put it on. The fit was perfect. Then he put on a pair of beaded mocassins and a brightly-coloured sash, the kind the halfbreed people wore in the early days. This he wrapped around his waist, letting the ends hang down. Next, his large silk bandana, which he put around his neck, and finally, a good blanket that he kept for special occasions, which he draped over his shoulder. Grandfather was now ready to go to the store. He took a bag, tied his door shut, and away he went down the road into the valley.

On this particular day there were many white people in and around the store. Some were swimming, others just lounging around. The store had a large verandah facing toward the lake. Many more white people were seated on the verandah, visiting and talking to each other, among them the local farm instructor and his wife. While these people were busy visiting, who should appear from around the corner but Grandfather. Grandfather always laughed when he told this part. He said, "I knew something was wrong because everybody stopped talking and looked at each other. Suddenly the farm instructor's wife jumped up and came over to me. She said, 'Good day Earth Man,' and something else which I didn't understand, then she took my hand and helped me up the steps and into the store. When I was in the store the farm instructor came over and took my other hand, then both of them led me to where the storekeeper was. He asked me what I wanted and I made a sign with my hand. The storekeeper knew right away what I wanted, as I had been there before and he knew me. As I made other purchases, the farm instructor put the goods into my bag. He was so helpful he kept getting in my way. I finished my selection and was about to pay, but he beat me to it. Other times when I went to the store I usually rested and visited the storekeeper, but not this time. The farm instructor was in a terrible hurry to help me out of the store and into a car. When we got to my house the farm instructor told me that I should not wear what I was wearing. I told him he was the one who said that this article was to be worn, but he said,

'No, no, Earth Man.' He made a sign that I was to wear it next to my skin and not on the outside. I knew then that I had embarrassed him and his wife. But he paid for my goods," said Grandfather, "and gave me a ride home. Without him I would have been tired, for it was a hot day."

This farm instructor, whose name was Tom Guest, was a great friend to Grandfather Earth Man. Even so, he was responsible for denying Grandfather's last request. Grandfather wanted to be wrapped in his blanket and laid in the earth as his name directed. Tom Guest arranged for what he considered a decent burial for his friend. Grandfather was buried in a coffin made from lumber paid for by Tom Guest.

These were the last days of Grandfather Earth Man, a hunter and storyteller who described the unbelievable hardships that his grandfather's people endured, and the land which he loved, where these events took place.

He was buried on a hill overlooking the west end of Crooked Lake on the original Shesheep Reserve, now part of the Sakimay Reserve in Saskatchewan.

PINAYZITT FAMILY TREE

Pinayzitt (Partridge Foot) had five sons with his wife, Eldest Twin Girl. They both died on the Strawberry Lake Territory.

The five sons of Pinayzitt (Partridge Foot) and their families:

Akeywakeywazee (Earth Man, Earth Elder). Married *Ogemaapeetung* (Sitting Lady Chief). They had a daughter, *Osowwaycekak* (Gives Yellow Light, named after lady moon), Hilda, who married Alec Pelltier of Cowessess Band, Saskatchewan.

Earth Man died on the Sakimay Reserve (1830–December 12, 1937). Sitting Lady Chief died on the Sakimay Reserve, Saskatchewan.

Osowoppshkez (Yellow Calf). Married an unknown woman from *Waywayscappo* Band. They had no offspring.

Yellow Calf died very old on the *Waywayscappo* Reserve (Rossburn, Manitoba).

Keshickashewaymingot (Blessed By the Sky). Married *Otunwayp* (To Rest in Journey) of the *Muscowpettung* Band in Saskatchewan. They had a daughter, *Nowqwaycapeewek* (Noonday Standing Lady), Harriet, who married Charlie Wolf (*Ogemamaeegun*) of the Turtle Mountains Chippewa Band.

Blessed By the Sky died very old, on the Sakimay Reserve in Saskatchewan. To Rest in Journey died on the Sakimay Reserve in 1931.

Akeyashewaymingot (Blessed By the Earth) *Sanquis* (Mink). Married *Shumance* of the Cypress Hills Band, Saskatchewan. They had two sons. *Macheeaniquot* (Floating Cloud, Old Boy *Sanquis*) who married *Shawwinipinaysek* (Southeast Thunderbird Lady),

Ruth Irene Isaac of the *Kahkewistahaw* Band, Saskatchewan. And *Kakeymawanokay* (Makes it Rain, Young Boy *Sanquis*) who married *Peetaweqway* (Prayer Offering Lady) of the Shesheep Band, Saskatchewan.

Blessed By the Earth died very old, on the Sakimay Reserve. *Shumance* died in the Sakimay Reserve in 1937.

Punnichiace (New Born Bird, John Bird). Married twice. His first wife was Emma Bird (maiden and Indian names unknown), and his second wife was Betsy Bird (maiden and Indian names unknown). He had one daughter with his first wife: *Sakaywayaniqadok* (Cloud Coming into View), Jean, who married Daniel Joseph Gayewish of the Clear Lake Band in Manitoba, and one daughter with his second wife: *Naynacwaypinayseek* (Martha Bird Huntinghawk), who married Peter Huntinghawk of the Rolling River Band in Manitoba.

New Born Bird died in middle age, January, 1906, on the Rolling River Reserve in Manitoba.

THE WANDERINGS OF PINAYZITT
AND HIS PEOPLE

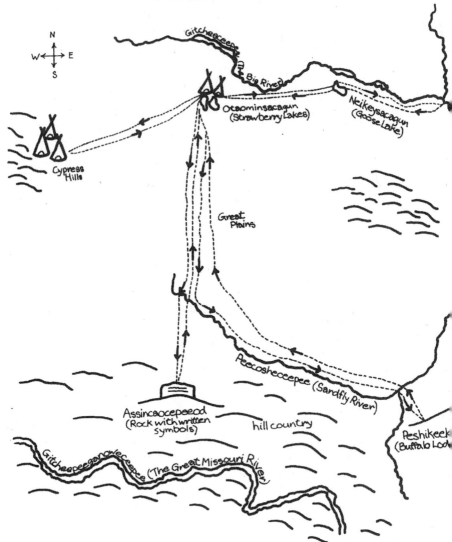

"To the west (Cypress Hills), we went to visit and to hunt. To the south, where Rock With Written Symbols is found, we went to fast and to pray. To the southeast, we went to Buffalo Lodge Hill where Grandfather Buffalo is found to seek his children. To the east, along the Big River we hunted as far as where the two rivers meet and go together to the east."

Akeywakeywazee
(Earth Elder)

THE LAST RAIDING VENTURE OF THE GRANDFATHERS

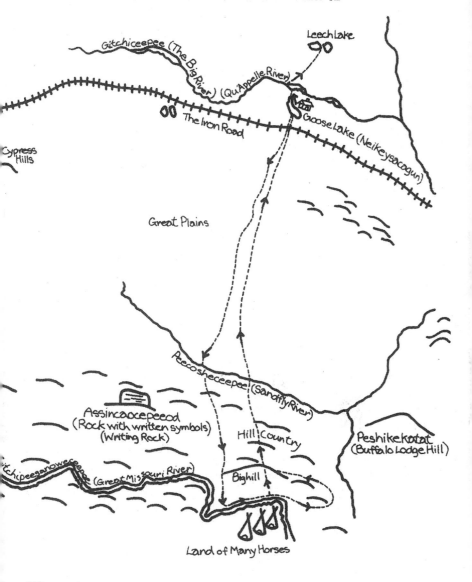

Leech Lake

Gitchiceepee (The Big River) (Qu'Appelle River)

The Iron Road

Goose Lake (Neikeysacogun)

Cypress Hills

Great Plains

Peecosheceepee (Sandfly River)

Assincaocepeeod (Rock with written symbols) (Writing Rock)

Hill Country

Peshikekotat (Buffalo Lodge Hill)

'tchipeeganowecepe (Great Missouri River)

Bighill

Land of Many Horses

"What was honorable in times past is now and in the future wrong because of commitment to a treaty as a people.

Osowoppshkez
(Yellow Calf)